# A Small Civilization

## Journal of a 7th grade classroom

*To Chris*

# CONTENTS

**Preface** ......................................................... 9

**Chapter One**
Finding Room 2103 ............................................. 13

**Chapter Two**
Starting the Mower ........................................... 23

**Chapter Three**
Puzzles ........................................................ 37

**Chapter Four**
True Grit ...................................................... 45

**Chapter Five**
In the Trenches ............................................... 60

**Chapter Six**
Belonging ...................................................... 73

**Chapter Seven**
Reading Dickens ............................................... 87

**Chapter Eight**
Into Deep Water ............................................... 98

**Chapter Nine**
What is Freedom? ............................................. 110

**Chapter Ten**

A Purple Heart ................................................................. 122

**Chapter Eleven**

Perspective ....................................................................... 138

**Chapter Twelve**

Being 13 .......................................................................... 145

**Chapter Thirteen**

Remember Me.................................................................... 161

**Acknowledgments** ........................................................ 175

I consider the two years in Beaufort when I taught high school as perhaps the happiest time of my life… No one had warned me that a teacher could fall so completely in love with his students that graduation seemed like the death of **a small civilization**.

—Pat Conroy, *A Lowcountry Heart: Reflections on a Writing Life*

# Preface

An apple for the teacher used to be the tradition, the cliché. I don't think I ever received an apple, but kids brought me all kinds of other things. Candy, lots of mugs, gift cards from Dunkin' Donuts. And don't get me started on the scented candles: oh-so-pungent pine, overwhelming cinnamon, and one labeled lavender that stopped your breathing. Then there were the special, heartfelt notes in the shaky or loopy handwriting of a boy or girl at the end of the year. I still keep many of those. I did not keep a note that arrived weirdly at the holidays, with a father's angry screed in black marker accompanying a wrapped box of coal. (Really; more on that later.) No other job I've had brought me gifts, especially ones like these.

That's one of the surprises that awaited me as I took a mid-career turn from other fields, mostly journalism, to become an English teacher in a public middle school. Over time I discovered more surprises. On the surface, I taught writing and literature, but underneath that I was deep into things I hadn't expected. When one girl confided to me that she felt like a "spy" in seventh grade, it instantly resonated. I realized I too was an eyewitness to a transformative stage of life, to kids in hand-to-hand combat with themselves and society's expectations, with the extraordinary realization that they had independent minds and could—

even must!—risk expressing their own original thoughts. Up so close, day-by-day at this pivotal stage, I watched them isolate personalities. Usually in slow-motion but occasionally in a burst that left me in awe, I glimpsed the metamorphosis that takes place in kids, physically, intellectually, hormonally, socially, magically—and sometimes tragically—right at this age. One writing prompt I gave them simply asked for a definition of "Being 13." They filled their journals: Responsibility. Anxiety. Freedom. Mood swings. Sleepovers. Drama (with a large exclamation mark). Maturity. Loss of childhood. Trying to belong. Independence. Cliques. Acne. Love. And on and on.

The words I've listed here are real, as are the events I'll tell about and the reactions and behind-the-scene comments, *sotto voce* or loud and furious, that I'll quote in the pages that follow. But I have to add a few caveats: Names have been changed, "to protect the innocent," as they used to say on that old TV police drama. While I've tried to show what it's like to be in the classroom as a seventh-grade year unfolds, there is some consolidation of events here, some blending of class years; and, with so many classes and many hundreds of kids, certain characters are partly composites. That said, everything you'll read here really did happen, even if this portrait is nothing like what you remember or think of as seventh grade.

There was another surprise, the most important, which took me a while to grasp. Going in, I had thought this job entailed entering into a contract with countless parties—parents and guardians, of course, but also society, and even the kids themselves—to transport precious cargo from Point A to Point B. In time, though, it became clear that the terms of such a contract didn't make sense. In seventh grade, more perhaps than in any other school year, I could not possibly deliver the same cargo from A to B. During the journey, the strangest, most startling shape-shifting happened among the passengers. That was a revelation to me, a challenge, sometimes a horror and, I must say, many times a delight.

That's what this book is about.

# ONE

# Finding Room 2103

Somehow, in my mellow middle-age years, I became a public school teacher for the first time. How did this happen? Why did I put myself in such a place at such a time? I had been a journalist who had enjoyed jobs as a newspaper reporter, magazine editor, off-and-on freelance writer, occasionally for *The New York Times*. Some of my offices had been in lofty and glamorous Manhattan perches. In some jobs, I had assistants to do my bidding.

Wouldn't becoming a public school teacher be moving backward? Surrounded by kids, wouldn't I long for adult company? With a schedule that hardly offered enough time for a bathroom break, wouldn't I feel trapped? Besides, wasn't it true that teachers had no real personalities? As a kid I often thought of the grownup in front of my classroom as remote, like a lighthouse.

Truth be told, all I'd ever wanted to be was a writer and a storyteller like my father. When my mother needed my younger siblings to behave on a car ride, she often asked me to tell them a story, which pleased me. I kept a diary as a kid, recording my feelings and even my dreams, as well as what I did each day. The reporting notebook my journalist father carried had a narrow, tan cover that said Steno in black letters. He could fit it in the breast pocket of his jacket when he went off to take notes for stories. I liked the names of the places he traveled to; names like Little Rock and New Orleans. When he came back he and my mother would have friends over and my siblings and I would fall asleep upstairs listening to his stories and the laughter that followed. That's exactly what I wanted to do, write and tell stories.

After college the only way to keep writing and get paid for it was to become a newspaper reporter. I wasn't particularly interested in news, but I loved writing features. And so I took notes and wrote stories about dull school board meetings, all the while hoping that my next assignment would be a profile of the intriguing homeless woman who walked up and down Dixie Highway. Later, when I moved on to magazine editing, I found myself out of my league on a staff of trend-conscious connoisseurs of pop culture. Not only was I less than conversant with the language, I didn't look the part. My sleek, fashion-conscious editor at a women's magazine sent her assistant to dress me up with a Vittadini scarf and suitably stunning earrings before calling me into a high-level meeting.

Back at home on the weekends, I wore overalls and put my hair in a bandana while my husband and I renovated an old farm house. We planted flowers and a vegetable garden and set up the rooms with "antique" trunks and desks and a church pew. I sewed the curtains. At heart, I was more of a thrift-store junkie.

At the magazine job I did enjoy the perks—dazzling views of Manhattan from the 17th floor, film previews, designer sales, expense account lunches, all kinds of swag. There were plenty of highs and, of course, some lows during a quarter century of navigating, pretty successfully, jobs that didn't exactly fit me, like a shoe a half size off. Still, making a change to teaching never entered my mind; even as an English major in college, I'd never considered becoming a teacher. That began to change as I watched our son, Jake, travel through grade school. More and more, I wanted to know what was going on behind the classroom door. This curiosity became most acute when he stopped talking to me at the age of 12.

At the end of every school day, all I could pry from the suddenly reticent boy I loved was one word, "fine." But at Open House, I was riveted by his English teacher in her stylish scarf (my old editor would have loved her), talking about the important class discussions, the books they would read and the journals they would fill. She was privy to coming-of-age talks that I would never hear.

Friends with older children told me not to worry, the real Jake would eventually resurface. That was all well and good, but the feature writer in me wanted to go behind the curtain and see for myself what was going on. My journalist husband, Chris, who knew how much I liked a good story, kept encouraging me to get inside this one, to think about becoming an English teacher. He told me I could make a difference, that kids would love me, that I would enjoy the stage—the "show business" aspect of it. "You're a natural," he said.

I could vaguely see the appeal of a teaching job. I thought about obstreperous kids revolting against the world and how I could help them express themselves. Or, for some overly sedate kids, I could stir things up. In any case, working from the inside, I might be able to help kids see writing the way I saw it, as a joyous liberation.

It was on a slow day of trying to peddle a freelance story—the merchandising side of my job was a bore—that I hung up the phone and sat still. I had recently recovered from a protracted struggle with Lyme disease, which had me mired in pain and lethargy and, for one frightening period, had even caused me trouble finding words. The slow pace of recuperation brought with it a new, critical look at my life. Freelance writing had become a very lonely business. I wanted to get back into a community. I wanted a new adventure. Why not at least try teaching?

By a miracle, I found a teacher's aide job in the second grade of Jake's old elementary school, right down the street from our Connecticut home. I packed a lunch and showed up on the first day. Within a week, the savvy teacher I was assigned to, who was even older than me (I'd just turned 50), treated me as an equal. The children fascinated me with their curiosity, honesty, tenderness and often hilarious behavior. My main assignment was to work with one lovable, bright boy on the autism spectrum; in doing so I drew him into a larger circle of kids, running interference when misunderstandings arose. Sometimes when we sat side-by-side in chairs at circle time, my darling seven-year-old charge would put his arm around my shoulder as if we were an old married couple.

I marched down the hall with a wiggly line of funny little kids. I squeezed into one of their tiny desks. I told stories, sang songs, and watched their eyes widen as I read to them. The way of life was fresh and impromptu each day. There were no dull meetings to cover. And, nobody ever asked, "Is that a Vittadini you're wearing?"

Chris had been right. I loved it. For the first time in my life, I experienced raw joy at work. When a pint-sized boy asked, "Want to watch me run?" and then burst across the playground, I knew I had never lived so perfectly in the center of the moment before. Honestly, I smiled so much that teachers up and down the hall asked me, "What are you taking?"

I never looked at the clock or the calendar as the seasons passed and recess went from sweaty jungle-gym activities to snowball fights. Each day I went in with the same enthusiasm, and soon it was June, time to see the kids pull their laminated names off the desks and fly out the door. I stood beside my teacher buddy with a tear in my eye. I didn't realize I was on the slippery slope.

"I miss them already," I whispered.

"There'll be another crop next year," she said, patting my shoulder.

I did it again the next year and as that second June approached, I set a new goal: to get a teaching certificate and have my own classroom. The state of Connecticut offered a crash course that prepared professionals from other careers to teach. I applied and, to my amazement, was accepted into The Alternative Route to Certification (ARC).

Along with other teacher trainees—former artists, lawyers, accountants, engineers—I read philosopher/educator John Dewey, studied psychology, delved eagerly into child development (a subject I had previously written about for parenting magazines), and learned laws governing special education. It was important to be conversant with those laws because children covered by special education plans would likely be in many of my classes.

We had stimulating discussions and challenged ourselves to compose thoughtful, personal reflections on educational theory. It was a jam-packed eleven weeks, the last half of which zeroed in on course material and lesson planning for middle school. I had wanted to return to elementary school, but that meant I'd have to teach math and science—not my strong suits—as well as writing and reading. I also ruled out high school, which struck me as a college-prep pressure-cooker. That left me with middle school. With a smile, I remembered that this journey had been inspired partly by the mystery of my son's seventh-grade year.

I did my practice teaching at an urban middle school in summer session—a last chance for kids who were in danger of failing seventh grade. A policeman roamed the halls with a walkie-talkie, keeping a special eye on the students with ankle bracelets. Unfazed, I flung myself into it, with poetry prompts, dramatic readings and journal writing. One girl told me she had nothing to write about because everything in her life was rotten. "Oh," I told her, "that makes for much better reading." Then I quoted writer Anne Lamott (something I would do over and over in the coming years): "Remember that you own what happened to you."

I sent her away, saying simply, "Tell your story."

A week later, she approached my desk with a provocative glare and thrust her first piece of writing at me. It described the time she and her mother discovered her mother's boyfriend hanging lifelessly from a ceiling fixture in his apartment.

Without blinking at the grisly image and struggling to keep my voice calm, I said, "Good, but can you offer more buildup to that moment?"

I was swept back into the world of telling stories, back into the newsroom, back to the magazine editing desk, back into the literature of real life. This was just what I wanted.

As that whirlwind summer was ending, I began looking for a real job in a real middle school. Brief as it had been, my training was almost over. Severely lacking in classroom know-how, I had the chutzpah to believe I could learn on the fly and I relished the opportunity to prove I could succeed. On my third interview, I found myself with a charming free-spirit of a principal who emerged from a back office in a muumuu with bare feet poking out. We chatted like old friends and soon she offered me a job—only a substitute position, filling in for a teacher on maternity leave, but it sounded perfect. The school—grades five through eight—was in the town next to where we lived. I would teach seventh grade "literacy," what we used to call English. I couldn't wait to see my room.

Custodians were preparing for the opening of school as I climbed an echoing staircase past empty classrooms and water fountains, looking for Room 2103. And there it was in a cul-de-sac at the end of a hall.

Turning the door handle, I took in my new "office." The walls were bare. A large metal teacher's desk sat in one corner while 25 laminate-topped student desks stood in rows with inverted chairs on top. Double-decker metal lockers, counters and cupboards filled the back wall, and a whiteboard covered the front one. I was glad to see a built-in bookcase.

Then I stood facing the best thing about Room 2103. Windows lined most of the far wall. They were west-facing and stretched from near the ceiling about two-thirds down. Beyond the expanse of glass, my eyes swam up to a huge, blue August sky. Spread below it, hardwoods and pines stretched away into a gentle Connecticut hillside. This opening to the world made the classroom seem immense. Like an island country. I pulled the shades up and locked them out of sight at the top so I could feel the sun on my face. My heart filled with a strange sense of promise.

I turned and noticed a narrow window in the door, just like the one I had imagined peeking through so long ago, to watch my own son join in class discussions and read and write in his journal when he was in seventh grade. Now I was on the *inside*.

Spinning around, I actually laughed out loud. In this room, I would not be the remote lighthouse as I'd thought of teachers when I was young. This bright place was the opposite of a rugged coast threatening shipwrecks. The sunlight streaming in suggested Life. Connection. A safe harbor.

I would be the teacher until the "real" teacher came back. For now, this was all mine. Almost immediately, though, that reverie burst with the realization: I was on my own. Could I actually pull this off? I knew it was important to exude an air of confidence. The thought nagged that I was an impostor, but I pushed it aside. Just maybe, I told myself, my experience in the world would give me an odd sort of advantage.

First order of business: I wanted my room to look like an elegant but fun library with books and art and sculpture. Raiding my son's bookshelves at home, I collected everything I could find that might appeal to seventh graders, then haunted yard sales and library sales for more. I brought in posters and paintings and clay busts, and bright metal sculptures. This room, I told myself, would dazzle every kid who entered it.

But, once again, my shiny bubble burst. Where were my instructions? As a late-summer hire, I hadn't been given detailed curriculum plans. Yes, there was a seventh-grade literature text and there were some writing goals. I knew there would be standardized tests and a need for regular report card grades along the way, but the steps in the middle were unclear. I wasn't sure how to write lesson plans. Hell, I didn't even know how to make a seating chart. This was like one of those classic bad dreams: It's final exam day, and you realize you've missed the whole semester. Again, that uncomfortable sense that I was an impostor.

But wait, I was just a substitute. Maybe those in charge just figured that when the "real" teacher returned everything would go back to normal. (As it would turn out, my across-the-hall neighbor, Shannon, also a seventh-grade English teacher, would generously share all kinds of tips.)

But I'm getting ahead here. Back to Room 2103. And suddenly… The First Day Of School.

My class lists waited on the podium. I watched the clock as the hands jumped to 7:45 a.m., the moment children would begin heading to homeroom. The pounding footsteps on the staircase caused an instant of panic. A loud herd of strangers was surging my way! OMG, I thought as I stood by the door to Room 2103. But I kept smiling, a little crazily.

All day long, waves of children—first for homeroom, then for five Literacy classes called "cores"—kept coming in and going out of the room as the bell rang over and over and I lost track of which class I was talking to. It was an out-of-body experience. The phone on my desk rang. It was one of the secretaries from the office calling to find out why I had never sent down the attendance list.

Taking attendance was a skill I would master, but very quickly I learned that such simple classroom mechanics were mere ripples on the ocean of interactions that make up a school day. Skillfully manipulating a non-compliant adolescent, for example, requires another order of mental dexterity.

In the book *Among Schoolchildren*, Tracy Kidder writes that a typical elementary school teacher must manage something like two hundred unpredictable "personal interactions" an hour. Perhaps seventh grade would demand fewer personal interactions than elementary school, but who could possibly prepare for such a challenge?

What would happen in my classroom, as it turned out, would be neither orderly nor predictable; the daily drama was intensified by the age and stage of the kids. I was teaching seventh grade. These weren't just any kids: These were kids, as I would learn, who were in the process of a profound metamorphosis.

If you study the literal process through which a caterpillar becomes a butterfly, you'll learn it's sticky. When the caterpillar reaches its equivalent of puberty it is overcome by hormonal changes that cause it to stop eating, hang itself upside-down, spin a cocoon and doze off. What happens next is creepy—it liquefies. To reemerge from its chrysalis as a new insect, the very tissues of the caterpillar need to change radically. The metamorphosis entails a total identity overhaul.

Okay, bizarre as it may be, that biology lesson (a science teacher friend related it, and it checks out) offered me a lens through which to study an analogous process for humans—the change from child to adult. It can look like a simple right turn in comparison, but is far more. Around the age of 12 or 13, which puts most kids in seventh grade, loving and attentive sons and daughters disappear and are replaced by aggravating, prickly strangers who roll their eyes and challenge everything, provoking even the mildest and most patient adults. Suffice it to say that young teens don't liquefy or get wings, but it's all too obvious they are in the awkward process of becoming something quite new.

I remember that the seventh-grade teacher with the scarf had watched my son go through this metamorphosis; surely it showed up in his writing and discussion. Seventh-grade English class: That's where this awkward but evolving creature, clamped into braces, sprouting pimples, honking and squeaking in speech, wrestles with a new physical and intellectual identity and begins to recognize a future self. In the classroom cocoon, a couple dozen 12- and 13-year-olds nudge each other through changes that often overwhelm them and make them defiant. As a sudden witness, I fielded their defiance as well as I could, urging my students to write through the growing pains. Some individuals led the way, breaking with tradition, rejecting conformity, taking a stand. On any given day, a brunette would arrive at school with green hair, a rule-follower would skip class, a pair of best friends would stop talking to each other. And through all this, individuals would begin to take shape.

And just as I would have felt when reading my own diaries, which I'd been keeping since I was their age—I felt so at home among my students' journals. Turn to any page in a seventh-grade English class journal and you'll likely see the unvarnished truth about all things. The crush, the wonder, the grief, the disappointment in self, the confusion about gender, the thirst, the drive, the prayers—all of it spilled onto the page. A small boy would write about his dreams of becoming tall and strong. A girl in his class would tell her journal about how she hated her changing body. These writers, enduring the turmoil of leaving child-hood behind, remained innocent and unselfconscious enough to blurt it out. The word that flashed in my head was "unguarded," which, of course, means open but also unprotected.

Whatever preconceived notions I'd had about what happens be-hind the classroom door and about my own preparedness dissolved when I was entrusted with these kids and witnessed their pain and their struggles, their rebound. Their metamorphosis.

But the last bell had rung that first day. It was too late to turn back. And I wouldn't have considered doing so even if I could.

# TWO

# Starting the Mower

In a journal entry about school, John Steinbeck echoed my own childhood dread: "I remember how grey and doleful Monday morning was…. What was to come next I knew, the dark corridors of the school …and the teachers, the weekend over, facing us with more horror than that with which we faced them."

As a child, I sensed that school was not exactly a friendly place. It felt like a forced march for both teachers and students. After kindergarten, where we mostly skipped to piano music and listened to stories, regimentation set in to the hum of those fluorescent lights that gave me a stomach ache. In third grade I had an old, stout teacher who kept reaching into the lower right-hand drawer of her desk for a small glass bottle. As the day went on, she got less and less concerned about what we did in class.

By fourth grade, the dull ache of school turned into agony: My four siblings and I were wrenched from the family seat in Atlanta and moved to New York where my father would take on an editorial position at *Newsweek*. Arriving in a suburb of Manhattan—elegant, leafy but completely unfamiliar—we looked and sounded as strange as a new life form. My Southern accent, saddle oxfords and habit of saying "yes ma'am" made the other students laugh out loud. They passed neatly folded notes among themselves. Recess meant standing alone on the blacktop watching sweaty children hurl a ball at each other. Sometimes the impact would knock a kid down (including, once, my older sister). Lunchtime was almost worse: There was the memory of walking toward an open seat and seeing a hand shoot out and a voice call out, "Saved." I dreaded each day, and never so much as when my Brooklyn-born teacher decided to take it upon herself to teach me how to pronounce words like b-a-l-l: "It's BAWWL."

Over the years, I put my school trauma in perspective, but the memories never totally went away. And so, when I had my own classroom, I was overcome with sympathy for the pale, distressed faces spread out before me on that "grey and doleful Monday morning."

If this was a prison for them, I sensed that my job was to shatter the walls, to bring air and light and warmth in the room. I pulled up the blinds, I opened the windows. If the woods outside distracted some of them, so be it. In came brightly colored ceramic pots of geraniums, red and pink and white, to line the windowsill. It was a start.

Right away, I could see kids respond: Shoulders relaxed, wrinkled brows smoothed out. When I put on a little music—maybe soft jazz, maybe Vivaldi, maybe The Temptations—the kids looked at each other in wonder. Even more so when, as I do sometimes, I suddenly burst out with a laugh that was a little too loud.

Even so, some clearly saw school as something to endure, to hold your breath and get through. They were simply serving time. Someday they would be paroled out "into the real world." Meanwhile each school day was spent breaking a certain pile of rocks.

My message was starkly different: It was not about preparing them for some far off "real world" that they would one day enter—it was about NOW. I wanted my kids to respond to this moment, insisting that what we did in class was both real and urgent. A deadline hovered. Without really thinking, I fell back on my training as a journalist.

Thirty years before, when I was 22 years old, I'd begun my professional life in the noisy, messy world of newspaper reporting—first at *The Greenville News* in South Carolina and then at *The Miami Herald.* We smoked cigarettes in the newsroom, swore way too much (a habit I'd definitely have to tame in the classroom), and hammered away on typewriters crowded onto littered desks, hurrying to meet deadlines with stories about bank robberies, corrupt politicians, municipal budgets—the exhilarating and the boring, back-to-back.

At the *Herald* I continued to cover education as I had in South Carolina, but some other things changed. I now drove a Triumph Spitfire convertible and had become fascinated by a guy on a competing paper who had a rich voice, a wonderfully serious expression, and who asked smart questions at press conferences. Within a year Chris Sullivan and I would marry. Over the years we moved a number of times as he followed jobs at the Associated Press, including to New York where I shifted to women's magazines.

I soon found that magazine staffers were mostly editors who came up with story ideas and shaped articles for each issue, relying on freelance writers. The rivalry in our intense brainstorming sessions high above Park Avenue or Broadway was exhilarating and very different from the atmosphere of the gritty newspaper world.

"So...? What do you have?" It was my imperious editor-in-chief. She loomed at the end of the table, taking in each of us lesser editors gathered for creative combat. She was tall and high-heeled, with silver-streaked hair pinned back and a couture suit perfectly fitted to her slender form. We were at *Woman's Day*, planning a July issue on a wintry morning in December (our lead time was about six months).

No one wanted to fail—or to go first. No one wanted to be waved away, hearing the editor-in-chief's curt, "No, no. That's been done."

At last someone suggested a summertime story that seemed innocuous, but it mirrored the thinking of our prudent, optimistic, cost-conscious reader: "An Unforgettable Vacation in Your Own Backyard." It invited a photo spread as well as party tips and recipes. And, it promised to be cheap! Heads turned. She smiled. If this cover line sounds prosaic, others that came out of this process were edgier or newsier.

"What else?" our editor pressed us. Then louder, "What else?"

One story idea proposed getting wealthy by quitting your job. (I've forgotten how that was supposed to work.) Another promised you could raise your kids' intelligence by, in effect, ignoring them. Once somebody took a chance with a profile idea: A Times Square minister who saved trafficked teenagers.

"Do it!" she commanded.

In the years ahead I moved on from magazines and learned even more about shaping and selling ideas when I began freelance writing after Jake was born. Working from home, I came up with ideas for assignments that would bring in income. I was selling words—as I would later tell my students. I could see their eyes flash (just as mine had earlier) at the dazzling notion that writers then typically earned a dollar a word. Just that concept could put a halo around a school writing assignment.

But, of course, in the classroom no one pays for words. Could I generate that old what-have-you-got urgency?

"What defines you?" I asked the kids with their marble composition notebooks open in front of them for daily journal writing.

"Who's got an idea?" Then I said it a little louder, "Who's got an idea?"

Looks of bewilderment. "Okay," I said, and clapped my hands. "Let's talk it through." My editor never did that.

"What do you mean?" asked a broad-shouldered boy with bristly, sandy-colored hair. As surreptitiously as I could, I checked the seating chart for his name.

"Well, Cameron, what makes you different from anyone else?" Cameron frowned. My prompt had been vague, but that was part of my psychology. I wasn't there to lead students by the hand; their classmates were. I noticed that in spite of all the head-shaking among them, some were beginning to write.

A hand went up. Eyes turned to a girl with a determined expression and heart-shaped face. I checked the seating chart again.

"Yes, Hannah," I said.

"I'm going to write about living in the shadow of my brother."

Kids straightened in their seats. They took in her clarity and confidence. I smiled. Approval.

"Shadow," I said, drawing the word out slowly. "Listen to what that word tells us."

I looked from face to face. "Everyone knows what it's like to be overshadowed, blocked from view. We know the sting of that experience wherever we've felt it: in a class, in a sport, in a family." I tapped Hannah's unopened notebook. Eyes followed my finger.

Cameron was still frowning, but others seemed to be beginning to understand the mechanics of this "give me something" brainstorming world.

Another hand went up. Seating chart check: "Yes, Jack O'Hara," I said, distinguishing him from the other Jack in the class.

"I'm going to write about playing baseball," he said. Everyone turned to me, as I used to watch for a glimmer on my editor's face. I thought of her saying peremptorily, "That's a topic. It's not a story or an angle."

"Okay, Jack. What about playing baseball?"

He turned his freckled face toward me but hesitated.

"What have you learned from baseball?" I asked. "Has baseball taught you something about yourself?"

Now more students were jotting in their journals. Some still gazed out our big window. Cameron squirmed uncomfortably. This was the beginning of the journey toward the deeper end of the pool. They were beginning to tell me—and themselves—who they were. Brainstorming helped students focus, but also brought everyone together. As we got better at this, kids would come up with ideas for each other. They'd share each other's successes. It's what you do in families, jobs, social groups.

This took time. At the beginning of the year, lots of students were more comfortable working independently, privately stacking up good grades. That was enough then. By the end, we would become a web of minds and shared imaginations, collaborating on short notice. Even though I was new at this, I knew from my hurried teacher training and from everything I had learned in the editorial world that this connection was essential.

So was my learning more about them. As my older sister Laurie, a deeply intuitive, out-of-the-box elementary school teacher, said, "To teach a kid, I have to know him first and openly admire some true part of him."

To that end, I asked the parents of my students to write a letter of introduction, if you will, for their son or daughter. Some of these letters were so tender and revealing.

"Joshua doesn't know it yet, but he is a great man. He's a natural leader with a deeper understanding of others than my daughters."

"Samantha is tied in knots trying to please everyone."

"Peter has a habit of not looking at you. Please be patient. He is trying. He just doesn't look like it."

If nothing else, these letters reminded me how varied childhoods can be. Some parents never wrote anything. Perhaps they had no time. No interest. No confidence. It told me something was missing.

I also gave each student an index card and asked them to describe three qualities about themselves or circumstances in their lives that would help me be a better teacher for them.

Amusingly, more than one noted the need for "kinesthetic" lessons. Apparently they had picked up educational jargon for: "Get me out of this desk and let me move around while I learn." Some admitted getting bored when teachers "talk a lot." (I talk a lot.)

But some wrote that their parents' divorce made it hard for them to be organized or that they had just moved here—from India, China, Brazil or even next-door New York State—and they didn't know anyone and felt lost. I could relate to that.

Luke just wrote: "My mother is in jail."

Full stop. There sat Luke in an oversized sweatshirt glaring at me. This dire revelation marked the beginning of a struggle between a bitterly angry and rejected child and a teacher who used every strategy she could conjure to gain his trust, tame his outbursts. I will never forget the day he followed me down the hall shouting defiantly and then slammed his fist against a brick wall, breaking a bone in his hand.

Kids like Luke made me question my naive goals about fully including each student. In fact, he would spend much of the year out of my classroom—with the counselor, or in the principal's office, or suspended. My relationship with him consisted mostly of emotional triage.

Of course I wanted all my kids to trust me enough to relax, breathe, speak and think. On the second or third day of school we played an ice-breaker game called "two truths and a lie." I would start by offering the kids two true statements about myself and a false one: "I have a husky dog, I once talked with the president of the United States, and I love sky-diving." (In fact, I had never been sky-diving).

The guessing game energized the atmosphere of the classroom, but it also taught us a little about each other. For the same reason, I would tell personal stories—about my school days, my dog, my son—when they suited the moment. Gradually, we became real people to each other. And our community, of course, was made up of quite an array of different individuals.

First, the boys: There were the everyday guys, not overly academic, not hyperactive, ready to do the best they could. Then came the athletes, mostly thinking about their next game; the immature pranksters goofing off to get attention; the highly competitive honor-roll regulars; the entertainers, bent on grabbing the attention of their classmates; finally the bored doodlers and the defiant ones.

We know from the books of family physician and psychologist Leonard Sax that stimulating boys' imagination requires some understanding of how they are different from girls. In *Why Gender Matters*, Sax writes, "We're not talking about small differences between the sexes, with lots of overlap. We're talking about large differences between the sexes, with no overlap at all."

Sax notes that from birth, boys are fascinated by movement—drawn more to a bouncing mobile than a human face. Anatomical retina differences between a boy's and a girl's eyes explain why girls are often drawn to color and texture while boys are more often attracted to location and movement.

Add to this that the hearing of boys is generally less acute than that of girls, and you have an uncomfortable fit in school. Boys sitting at the back of the room often have trouble hearing the typical voice of a female teacher; as a result they may look away, appear inattentive and get in trouble. Fortunately, I tend to project when I speak and I have a deeper voice than some women.

And being the mother of a son, I like to get kids up and moving as they are learning. That's why in my class, boys and girls learn prepositions by acting them out.

"Please get UNDER the table," I asked Buddy, knowing he would love just that kind of attention. He scrambled to his feet, knocking his water bottle flying and bumping his neighbor's desk in his haste to get under the table.

While he sat there grinning, I turned to the class.

"Hmm. If I were to say, 'Buddy is under the table'—who can tell me which word is the preposition?"

"UNDER!" Someone called out.

I turned to a dreamy-eyed boy watching leaves flip back and forth on the trees outside the window.

"Caleb, please lie OVER this stool." I backed away to give Caleb plenty of room in case he body-surfed to the other side. As this now-focussed boy draped himself over the stool, I called for the preposition and kids shouted it back.

Girls liked this too. Lindsey, a star soccer player, responding to my request to lean AGAINST a locker, sauntered across the room, her ponytail swinging, and eased herself against the metal locker. She folded her arms and cocked her head at the class. Some seventh graders relish the chance to show off.

Before I could even finish my question, voices chorused, "AGAINST!"

Once we were all clear about this particular part of speech, I'd slip in an impromptu "test." With no warning, I would call out "Preposition Positions!" and kids would hustle about, moving themselves under, over and behind things. Eventually some of them would even recite two dozen prepositions in alphabetical order, although I never asked them to memorize the list.

Learning parts of speech was one thing. But when it came to sitting down and writing essays, boys were handicapped by more than their bounciness. A wide array of research indicates that the part of the brain that governs language develops differently in girls and boys, with boys developing later when it comes to abstractions like "living in the shadow" of a sibling. So, when asked to write at a higher standard in seventh grade, boys more often got stuck. What to do? I went back in my mind to someone who understood hurdles in language processing. My journalist father, Bill Emerson, had become a university professor of writing late in life. I talked to him many times about teaching. I also remember an interview he once gave, about overcoming the most basic of teaching challenges. Talking in his unique way, he had a lot to say.

"You try to understand what's going on in your own mind and translate the process for the student. Sometimes you have a mortal struggle with the student's mind. It's combat. It's exhausting."

He went on: "Sometimes you can teach them broad techniques, the same way you can teach someone to foxtrot, pushing them through the steps, heaving them around the floor. But what you are trying to do is get them to move off on their own, creatively."

He found an even richer analogy: "It's like trying to start a reluctant lawnmower. You pull the cord and nothing happens. So you pull it and pull it and pull it. Finally, it kicks off."

That was the thrill of teaching: "The real thing is to see the awakening, the transaction begin in the mind, the spark jump…the motor start."

And he talked about something else—"the student who will be a writer." This would not be the one who wrote tidy, neat paragraphs. "I'm interested in the untidy student, the obsessive student who has nightmares, who questions the world around him. Students that have had something happen to them."

So, back to teaching writing to the kids in my class. Let me focus briefly on two boys and two girls. First, Will, a silent boy with slicked back hair and an expression that clearly suggested he was serving a mandatory sentence attending school.

The writing prompt was, "Write about something you care about." Blank face. I knelt by his desk. We talked. After a while he showed me a business card with his name on it. It turned out Will was an entrepreneur.

"What do you do?" I asked.

"Cut grass. I have 23 clients."

Astonishingly he was running a lawn maintenance business and had made enough money to buy a riding mower, transported on his uncle's trailer.

"Can I write about that?" I took a breath. Hell yes! I thought.

Aloud, I said, "Sure. Let's make this come alive."

With a fresh sheet of paper, he started and steadily mowed along, down to the bottom, disappearing into his writing, explaining his passion.

"Reading this, I can almost smell the new-cut grass," I said. In class we'd talked about the importance of including sensory details.

"I can smell it, too," he said, then put his head down and kept writing.

An outsider had become an insider in both ways: I was in his world, he in mine. And this was not about grass, in the end, but about trust.

But sometimes a safe environment is not enough. Sometimes there's an obstacle like a fallen tree limb across the path. This was the case with Richard, a slightly disheveled boy who stared at the prompt on the whiteboard. After a couple of my questions, he turned his hooded eyes to me and spoke just above a whisper.

"There is only one thing I can write about," he said, "and I can't write about it."

I didn't know what that burden was, and I didn't want to pry. After a minute I began. "Sometimes you don't have to address a subject head-on. Can you write up to it?" He shook his head.

Another minute passed. Then I was the one whispering: "What is it?"

He turned a furrowed brow toward me.

"My dad died."

Oh. I rejected an inclination to pat his shoulder.

"You will write about it someday," I said, gently. "Ultimately, it will be helpful for you to write about it." We were quiet for a moment.

"Pick one memory," I said, "that you hold clearly in your mind. Write that truly. Consider this a long-term project."

Richard stared at me and then at the marble notebook and the pencil. "Can I use a computer instead of writing by hand?"

I nodded. Head bent over the keyboard, he began to wade into the shallow end of his sea of sadness, staring out toward the darker depths.

The memory Richard picked was about a car ride with his father, talking about the Yankees. It wasn't long before he went deeper. "When I look back at the time I spent with him," he wrote, "everything is like a video with no sound, just simple things and very few of them...like playing catch." He wrote about some things he couldn't remember, like the sound of his father's voice.

As Richard and even Will reminded me, the assembled writers in a seventh grade English class, boys and girls, are often working on missions of self-discovery. It became obvious that I needed to help them muster the will to go as far they could go.

If teaching boys calls for more out-of-the-box strategies, teaching girls this age sometimes demands running interference. Remember Dr. Sax? His research shows girls favor colors and often can sit still for longer periods of time and tend to focus on relationships. The key word here is relationships: the quest for friendship or love.

Emotions can run so high, especially for girls who are sometimes as fragile as blown glass. So the stage is set at an age when peer pressure is at its height and opportunities like Facebook, Snapchat and Instagram stand ready to expose kids to electronic bullying and social sabotage. Lunch groups dominate social ranking, and revolving crushes cause near cardiac emergencies. We called the whole thing DRAMA.

Of course in my classes there were girls who were largely immune: grade-oriented kids who did their work and moved on; inspired individuals immersed in a passion for writing, reading, art, music; and goth types who traveled in their own tight circle. These girls helped provide ballast for our ship on a stormy sea.

In contrast, Hailey was the high priestess of boy craziness. Holding court in her ripped jeans, lip gloss and Victoria's Secret underpinnings, Hailey defined my challenge. How could I find an intellectual path to this winsome, happy and confident girl who was also oblivious of the fact that she was in school? She and her thicket of girlfriends chattered and squealed over boys as if class were a reality dating show.

"Hi, Ms. Sullivan," Hailey greeted me melodiously each day before settling in for an hour of flipping her long auburn hair and sending Snapchat messages furtively inside her desk. She looked up periodically to flash a warm smile my way.

I strolled by, held out my hand and took her phone, again.

"Ohhhhh," she moaned. "When will I get it back?"

She knew it was bound for the principal's office, where she could reclaim it at the end of the day, but she was hoping for a miracle.

Whenever she put pen to paper, Hailey could write for an hour in rounded letters, line after line, which I found very encouraging until I read what she wrote. No matter the assignment, Hailey wrote about her friends and slumber parties and cute boys and favorite food. When the assignment directed her to describe a meaningful event that changed her life, she wrote five pages about a birthday party.

At the other end of the girl spectrum was Patricia, an introverted girl who sat alone at lunch. She was an island of tangled hair and cloudy glasses.

For a teacher it is a tricky challenge to reach a kid whose main survival technique is to shut down. One day I stopped by Patricia's desk to check her homework, and she buried her face in her T-shirt. When I asked about her missing assignment, tears welled in her eyes. When I crouched to whisper encouragement and calming words; she turned her head the other way.

I had no starting point. She never spoke. She rarely wrote anything. I called her parents for help. They were divorced and she divided the week between the two homes, living with her mother for several days and then her father. I learned that some of her step-siblings bullied her.

"She doesn't care about school," her father said. He didn't know what to suggest.

Back in the classroom Patricia's misery haunted me. I called home again and left a message. Her father called back that evening just as I had reached the grocery store, and I sat in the parking lot for half an hour getting information I wished I'd had earlier. The problem had started long before the divorce.

Patricia entered the world as a four-pound preemie. She hadn't learned to walk or speak on time and as a result couldn't play with other children her age. Life had been one long struggle to survive and fit in. She measured herself against her older sister who could do "everything." Finally, her father added, "Patricia thinks she's stupid."

Whoa. Her family had not volunteered these details in their letter about her. As with Luke, the boy whose mother was in jail, this was a triage situation. For the time being, I kept an eye on Patricia, but stopped expecting too much. As with fatherless Richard, I'd give her time.

# THREE

# Puzzles

*Thirteen's no age at all. Thirteen is nothing.*

With these words, the poet Phyllis McGinley did not mean to dismiss the age. She meant that 13 is a no-man's-land. The dictionary calls such a place "an area of unowned, unclaimed, or uninhabited land." It's a place in-between. Those of younger years dwell under the roof of childhood. Beyond 13 lies the universe of adulthood.

McGinley went on:

> *Thirteen...*
> *Has secrets from itself, friends it despises;*
> *Admits none to the terrors that it feels;*
> *Owns half a hundred masks but no disguises;*
> *And walks upon its heels.*

McGinley won a Pulitzer Prize for verse that is thoughtful, serious, analytic yet often tinged with an element of lightness. Take the title of this poem, "Portrait of Girl with Comic Book." Reading it, I wondered about the source of McGinley's insight. Turns out that besides being a poet she had been a junior high English teacher. Like me, she experienced 13 twice—the second time as a determined, not to say detached, observer.

*...half a hundred masks but no disguises.*

I wanted to get behind those masks in my classroom. One assignment was a question (a "metacognitive" one, in modern educator's jargon) exploring how the act of writing made students feel. Each was asked to complete the sentence, "When I write I..."

Some kids began immediately to describe what might be labeled writer's block; one felt "a clot in my brain." But others described writing as power. One girl wrote, "When I write I feel like I have been allowed to walk into a wide open field and I am free."

Hailey gushed: "When I write I love, love, love it. It lets me describe my friends and what we do together."

And Patricia? There was no entry in her journal.

Working nearby, Amir was pressing down hard on the paper, so hard his pencil tore it. After "When I write I..." he scrawled two black words.

"HATE IT."

Amir. What would I do with this boy? Checking his record, I learned he had received 30 recorded disciplinary actions over the previous two years. He'd been sent out of class, kicked off the bus, ordered out of the lunchroom. His anger simmered right below the surface, from each morning's Pledge of Allegiance to the arrival of buses at the end of the day. Yes, he hated to write. He also hated to read or to participate in class discussions, sighing or groaning at such times. His journal entries, when he made any, were doodles.

After students finished describing their reactions to writing, we talked about our different attitudes. I made it clear that there was no judgment here. Everyone had different experiences that we could benefit from. Both those who loved writing and those who hated it really made an effort to talk it through.

Except for Amir. He ignored it all, leaning over in an exaggerated way to retie his sneakers, first one, then the other, slowly, his whole body facing down.

I had a hunch that Amir held back because he knew he wasn't good at reading and writing and didn't want to be ridiculed. I knew I needed some guidance to be able to help him. After school, I went down to the first floor classroom of a fellow teacher, Deborah, who had become my mentor.

In fact, she had been formally given that role when the teacher I was temporarily replacing as a substitute decided not to come back. Now that I was the "real" teacher I could get help. This eighth grade English teacher became my North Star in all things academic, philosophical and practical.

Deborah, who held an Ivy League PhD, had persuaded the school administration that failing students often fall behind due to weak reading skills and will only plunge further unless we can catch them. She designed a course that focussed on strategic reading and it became a part of our standard curriculum—offering struggling seventh- and eighth-graders a second dose of English in place of a foreign language.

Deborah's colleagues considered her an academic yogic. She became known for the phrase, "Give it the time it deserves." That was her counsel whenever we got hysterical over what we considered unnecessary checklists and other bureaucratic chores that temporarily swept into vogue. She meant: Rely on your own good sense; weigh the value of any directive and treat it accordingly.

So, when Amir wrote "hate it" I went to see Deborah. I wanted her to test him to see if he would qualify for her catch-up class. When Amir's reading score, though in the low-average range, proved to be too high to qualify for her class, Deborah took him anyway. That was partly at my pleading, partly because she knew a kid like Amir needed close attention. Planning some lessons together, but working separately, Deborah and I double-teamed our struggling learners by reinforcing skills. When Deborah worked on a specific skill Monday, I would draw it out of students in my class Tuesday, rigging it so the remedial kids could shine.

From his "hate it" day onward, I searched for insight into Amir's life and personality. During one silent reading time, I saw him idly wander over to a bookcase and stand facing it. When I joined him, I noticed his gaze had settled on a jigsaw puzzle in a box on the top shelf. I took the box down, put it on a table obscured from the class, and asked if he'd like to work on the puzzle instead of reading. Never mind the rules, I thought.

Amir nodded. Opening the box quietly, since I didn't want the other kids to know what was going on, I began to lift pieces out by the handful, spreading them on the table, face-up. Once the box was empty, I tipped it up so we could see the picture of the completed puzzle and I began grouping pieces by color.

"No," Amir said. "We do the edges first."

Scanning the table, he plucked a piece and in no time completed the top, then moved on to the left edge. He had an unerring eye for shapes and subtle changes of color. "My mother and I do puzzles," was all he said.

The next day he asked me in a whisper if he could work on the puzzle again. Though no one was supposed to be off the hook during reading time, I nodded. For half an hour he worked away. For the first time, there was a peacefulness surrounding him.

I was learning more about this boy. His father had abandoned the family when Amir was very young, and his mother, an immigrant from Egypt, spoke English haltingly—and bitterly, sometimes cursing on phone calls with me. Her grade-school education precluded any chance of a high-paying job. She raised her son on resentment.

By the time Amir had completed the puzzle, I had come up with another idea. During study hall, I led him to a framed magnetized board attached to the wall and handed him a box full of words printed on magnet strips.

"Want to write a poem with these?" I asked.

Reaching into the box he pulled out a strip displaying the word "butterfly." Then another that read "milkshake" and a third that said "swim." The absurdity made him smile. I pulled a stool over to the board and left him to the random magic of creating nonsense verse. When I returned, he had assembled 10 lines of "poetry." He was so intent on choosing words he didn't notice me.

Gradually, Amir lowered his guard. He began to listen to class discussions. I watched his face and could tell he was reacting to ideas he heard. He wanted to speak sometimes; I knew he did. Haltingly, too, he began writing in his journal. When I checked it now, I found coherent thoughts and even some opinions.

In time, Amir stopped making fists; his shoulders seemed more relaxed. Maybe he was ready for some feedback. One day I assigned each student a partner to share their journal writing on the prompt: "Describe an event that changed the way you saw the world."

On an impulse, I paired Amir with Bronwyn. She was a serene, artistic girl, one of the brightest in the class. At a college-level she read online books on futuristic themes, hundreds of pages at a time. Among her many interests, Bronwyn was passionate about protecting the environment. Her creamy complexion and wire-rim glasses suggested a face from another time, maybe one of the sisters in *Little Women*. Whenever I introduced a new idea to the class, my eyes often sought her out, looking for signs of recognition or connection. She became my touchstone.

When I announced that she and Amir were partners, her eyes instantly widened in alarm. She was not scared of Amir; she was scared of embarrassing him. He might not have anything to share or discuss.

Above all, Bronwyn didn't want to be part of making anyone look or feel bad.

"It's okay," I said quietly, as I passed her desk. "Prepare to meet another mind. He's ready." I suppressed my own flicker of doubt about that.

Already, I had scanned Amir's journal entry, reading words that only a Bronwyn could hold as gently as they needed to be held. He'd started with these sentences: "I realized I wasn't important in the world. I realized I didn't matter on the day my father got in the car and drove away. He didn't look back. And he never came back."

Around the room, pairs of students were reading to each other from their journals and discussing what they revealed. I stayed away from Bronwyn and Amir but never stopped watching them. Even from the edges of the room, I could see her composed face leaning in to read softly from her writing. Clearly, Amir was listening. When she finished, he read his words to her intent face. As I got closer, I could hear his husky voice and see his finger following his own penciled lines of writing. She listened with a tilted head, her face flushed and her eyes shining.

At the end of class, when most students had left, Bronwyn carefully returned her journal to the bucket on the table by the door where I was standing.

"I was surprised he let me see his vulnerability," she said very softly as I nodded. "His words were so beautiful," she said, "and so painful."

After school, I dropped by Deborah's room to tell her about the episode. I was really excited. Deborah was cool, as usual.

"He can succeed," she said evenly. "The same thing is happening with him in my class." She felt sure Amir would be ready to move on to a foreign language next year. No fanfare, no bottle rockets. Just steady faith and steady progress.

Before class the next morning, my phone rang. It was Dave, the principal. (He had succeeded the principal with the muumuu who'd hired me.) Dave had received a call from Bronwyn's father. We needed to talk.

Uh-oh, I thought. I'm going to get it for pairing this gentle monarch butterfly with the toughest kid in the class. Had I gone too far this time? As I walked down the hall, I started marshaling my defense. I had monitored this shared reading exercise, after all. Bronwyn hadn't complained to me, not really. It had all seemed peaceful, right? Besides, no one but Bronwyn could handle this delicate situation; at the time I was fairly sure it would be okay.

When I got to his office, Dave ushered me in, closed the door and repeated that Bronwyn's father had phoned. "He wanted to talk about his daughter's reaction to something that happened in your class yesterday," he said. "It involved Amir."

The name jangled in my brain, suddenly a jarring sound. Though I had come to know a different boy, the word "Amir" was a proper noun that every teacher equated with trouble. The parents knew this as well as their kids. My palms were sweating.

"I must say I was surprised at what he told me," Dave said, studying my face. My heart thudded in my ears. "His daughter told him that in all the years she has shared a class with Amir, she's only seen him treated as a delinquent—never like a human being. In fact, she was completely surprised, he said, when her teacher asked her to read Amir's writing and talk with him about it. She told her father she was grateful for that."

Dave paused for a moment, then said, "You know what Bronwyn's father called you? 'A true teacher.'"

Many things were going through my head as I opened Dave's door and walked out. Strangely, one of them was the word "transaction." In our teacher training I remembered that John Dewey used that word to describe what education should be. Was the Bronwyn/Amir moment what he was trying to get us to understand with that clunky term? Of course the father's comment also echoed in my head: "A true teacher."

When I started my new career, as I've mentioned, I'd worried that I was an impostor—in part because I operated on instinct, like the instinct to put those two together to share their journals. A true teacher. Maybe in this world my instinct could be an asset.

Passing through the main office, I saw Hailey trying to negotiate the release of her cell phone from Celeste, our battle-weary school secretary.

"End of the day," Celeste repeated. "Not until." Hailey put on her sweetest smile.

"I'll keep it turned off," she promised.

The secretary returned the smile.

"Sure you will. Still, no. Now go on to homeroom before you're late."

# FOUR

# True Grit

I was learning from my mistakes, as well as my occasional successes. More and more, I was trusting my intuition. Still, as an outsider, I was often aware of how unfamiliar I was with the modern education system, the world outside my classroom, the business of school. For one thing, it had its own language. Teachers used an alphabet soup of acronyms—SPED, IEP, SLO, WISC, CCSS—like common nouns in everyday conversation. As soon as I learned one, another one popped up. What were they saying? I was reluctant to ask.

This strange jargon was everywhere, in our small weekly team meetings and spinning through the large monthly faculty gatherings. But sometimes it wasn't the language that confused me, it was a nonsensical idea. Let me focus on one meeting.

That day, as we dragged ourselves down the long hallways to the small amphitheater, Donnell joined me, coat on, eager to leave.

"I don't have time for this Mickey Mouse crap," she grumbled. After 33 years of teaching, Donnell had long since stopped mincing words.

Once inside, I joined Anna, my sixth grade counterpart, and nodded back over a row of seats to my mentor, Deborah, who was wearing her union negotiator hat at that moment, listening for any requirements from the principal that might conflict with our contract. Libby, my Spanish-teaching and wine-drinking buddy, was on the aisle for a quick departure.

Our principal, Dave, was a jocular guy whom most of us liked, and he stood at the front, calling out greetings. My memory of what happened on that day consists primarily of vague feelings of dismay. There might have been a motivational presentation, maybe an inspiring video. I don't remember exactly.

After we'd all settled in, Dave began what we could quickly tell would be a pep talk. He didn't directly mention what he was likely thinking about—such as the standardized test results showing this grade was up and that one down, scores that, we knew, ranked us as teachers, classroom by classroom. He didn't talk about "data walls" or the "electronic gradebook" posted for parents, or other modes of daily measurement that we were increasingly conscious of. Instead, he said he recognized how difficult our jobs were. He used words like "courage," "drive," and "confidence," throwing in a few fist pumps for emphasis.

Old-timers crossed their arms. Twenty-somethings glanced up from their phones momentarily, leaving Instagram or Facebook to roll their eyes.

Finally, he got to a catchphrase that we supposed was passed along from the superintendent's office: "As educators, our job is to help our students develop more—(long pause for dramatic effective)—GRIT."

Grit?

Dave went on about kids being led over an obstacle course with us upfront, urging them along. My own mind drifted to an image of a climber with an ice axe, inching determinedly upward on a steep snow-bound slope, the strains of "Climb Every Mountain" from *The Sound of Music* rising to a crescendo.

A groan from Donnell snapped me back to the room. I noticed others squirming. We could hear the second hand on the wall clock. Then, thank God, another voice.

"Dave, c'mon! Are you kiddin' me?" Ally barked in her Brooklyn accent. She was a gym teacher. We all laughed.

"These kids can't do a push-up!" More laughter. She was rolling. "Hell, more than half of 'em wear Velcro sneakers 'cause they can't make the effort to learn to tie shoelaces." (To myself, I thought: They won't be climbing mountains in Velcro sneakers.) Even Dave started to smile.

Grit? Later I learned that the idea of teaching students to "develop grit" was trending and that some high school teachers were even testing kids for it and trying to use a scale to measure it. To my middle-school teacher's mind, the notion that a teacher could conjure grit irritated me. Grit represented a state of mind, an attitude developed through practice. It came from the inside. Dave's efforts were well-meaning and probably pretty harmless, but the simplistic grit message felt packaged. Meetings like these felt like such a waste of time.

On the other hand, though, the new teacher in me couldn't help marveling at the constructiveness of many of our other group discussions. Previous businesses I'd been part of were built on competition. But public education, at its best, seemed more like a large, well-trained army whose mission was ultimately to move all our kids to higher ground, while always preserving the individuality of each soldier.

A different kind of in-school meeting first made me see this back when I was working as a teacher's aide in second grade. I remember getting goose bumps as I listened to six highly-credentialed adults around a table, struggling to pinpoint and untangle the challenges facing a single small child.

Meetings—the constructive ones, and even the droning ones with silly mandates—often became fodder for helpful conversations with my younger sister, Ellen. She knew I kept journal notes and insisted I send her regular updates of classroom scenes and other teaching experiences, even details of meetings. An artist and yoga instructor, she enjoyed using her outsider's lens to deconstruct, analyze and philosophize.

My instinctive, out-of-the box efforts to light a fire under my students were well known to Ellen. In fact, she had given me a squawk box that could emit a drum roll, a snort or a Bronx cheer—not to mention applause or maniacal laughter—which I activated from my pocket whenever I needed to stir things up in class. The one thing I could not tolerate was boredom, theirs or mine. Once I had them awake I could move on to my real goal—for them to learn, to set and meet a high standard, to value excellence.

I remembered what Richard, one of my brightest students, had said earlier on the day we got the "grit" talk. With a brief glance, he had looked at the B-minus he'd received on his essay and stuffed the paper into a folder. Here was a fine writer brought down by a dozen careless mistakes, including basic punctuation and capitalization errors. "Well," he'd said, "it's not that bad."

I took a long look at the mannish, six-foot-tall kid. I knew his life had been a struggle since he'd lost his father. I had watched him slip into a disturbing apathy from time to time. But this particular display of indifference, for some reason, brought me up short.

"Not that bad?!" While he stared at me, an idea was born.

"Is it better than a sixth-grader could do?" I asked.

He shrugged, but now I had his attention.

"Let's print it out again and send the uncorrected version down to sixth grade and see how many errors they can find," I suggested.

In an email to Anna, I related the story and attached the essay, removing Richard's name. She immediately picked up on the potential of this "real life copy-editing job" for her kids. "They love to find other people's mistakes," she said.

The results of the error hunt were dazzling. When we got it back, Richard's page was on fire with neon highlighter marks, explained by margin notes in Anna's hand.

He read it silently, with a wrinkled brow. "Okay. I could have caught some of these."

Not exactly a victory, but he did promise to try harder the next time. Was this a hint of grit? Maybe. But how to inspire grit in another kid who complains about, say, having to read "a whole chapter" in an assigned novel? Or the one who simply closes the book, blandly sighing, "I don't really like it that much."

That one closing the book was Lindsey. Wait a minute, I thought. Wasn't Lindsey a standout soccer player? Sports demand grit, right? Lots of my kids played on teams. Surely they tried again after failing on the field. And again, and again. They were driven by something inside them, which again is how I conceived of grit. I watched Lindsey put her pencil down, and half-heartedly explain that she'd run out of ideas for responding to my prompt about a theme in the book. She slid down in her seat.

"So," I asked, my voice as cool as I could keep it, "you've decided to quit?" Other students looked up.

"Do you play a sport?" I asked her. Of course I knew she did.

"Yes," she said, flipping her ponytail. "Soccer."

"How do you respond when your coach gives you a direction?"

"I follow it." Lindsey was beginning to see where this was going.

Scanning the room, front to back, my glance swept over all of the athletes, musicians, dancers, artists and singers, all the gamers, martial arts students—everybody. It was obvious to them that I was addressing the entire class.

"Let's talk about effort. All of you, whether you have a coach or some other leader—for your sport, your music, your dance, your art— you all do your best even when you're tired and even when you're not being so successful, right?"

A dozen heads nodded. I looked at the red-rimmed eyes of Chaz, the champion swimmer; at Jack, the baseball player; at Mae, the exhausted pianist who traveled each week from our Connecticut town to Lincoln Center in New York City to study piano.

"Well, this is for all of you: I am your English coach," I said. They waited. Kids looked back and forth at each other.

"I don't expect you to write brilliant prose every time you put a pencil to paper. I don't expect you to get an A on every assignment." I spoke softly. I didn't mention grit.

"But I do expect you to write your heart out." I stared into one set of eyes and then another. "I expect you to get tired trying." My voice got firmer, a little louder.

"And I expect you to get better and better and better just like you do in your sport or art. Nothing that's really worth working for is going to be easy. But you know that."

The swimmer was smiling and so was the pianist. Lindsey gave a curt nod and opened her journal.

I have given this speech many times: Education is like sports; you will only get out of it what you put in; you may learn more from losing than from winning. And so on. The "coach" speech works—up to a point. But over time I came to realize it's an imperfect metaphor. A loss on the playing field is different from losing in the classroom, where a failing grade belongs only to the student. No one says "good try" when you get an F. Losing on a report card is just plain losing. And it won't be tolerated at home.

Some students steam in their own personal pressure cooker at home, bombarded by scores from their classes popping up in the digital grade-book. Some parents even set their phones to ping each time a grade is published, and they use these scores, even trivial ones, as a yardstick for their children. Today's might be just a vocabulary quiz worth only a few points, but tonight, in the parents's eyes, it might loom like an SAT score.

Less competitive children watch their parents blast emails at their teachers. Others, like Cameron, pester teachers relentlessly about every point they lose on a quiz. "My parents are going to kill me," Cameron would say.

Our obsession with high test scores is one of the "corrosive forces in American life," writes author and teacher William Zinsser, who published a popular article in a national magazine 50 years ago pleading for a freedom Americans don't have—the right to fail. Zinsser believed that we "paralyze" our young people by demanding that "every step be a step up to the next rung on the ladder."

This misplaced angst was one reason I didn't put grades on their journals. Mainly, I wanted kids to write from the heart, whether my prompts were general, such as, "What makes you different?" or quite specific, such as the one I assigned on the anniversary of the September 11th terrorist attacks that happened years earlier when the writers were children. Our little town was a commuter train ride away from the obliterated World Trade Center.

One girl, calling up that distant memory, wrote: "I sat near a window and kept staring out. I was terrified a plane would fly into our school." But many others had only fuzzy memories, feelings, impressions, and little grasp of the big picture. I imagined these writers as Faulknerian narrators who didn't understand the story they themselves told. I tried to help them realize this could be a chance to evaluate the narrator's perspective.

"I was picked up before school was over, and in the car the radio was turned off. My mother had been crying," one student wrote.

"My father was at home, sitting on the sofa watching the television," another remembered. "I had never seen my father at home during the day."

Later, some of them learned that their aunts, uncles, godparents, and neighbors had been close to or even at the scene of the disaster in New York. They had responded as firemen or had been heading toward the building from the subway or were watching from a nearby building.

Some didn't survive.

This sort of journal writing almost always inspired class discussions where kids learned about each other. And I learned about them. For example, what lingering fears did they have about unexplained violence that came so close to home?

I would find out for myself one day in December before winter break. I thought I was prepared for the usual restlessness that sets in as holidays approach, but that morning I struggled to keep order in class. Clearly, something was palpably awry. First two phones went off in quick succession. I began to get impatient. A boy sheepishly apologized.

"It's my mom," he said. "She's coming to get me early."

For the umpteenth time I found myself wondering: Why can't parents plan their holiday trips within the parameters of school breaks? Is it really that hard?

A girl who always did the right thing moved quickly to silence her ringing phone, but this interruption seemed to set off chattering and whispering up and down the rows.

"Okay, come on, guys," I said. "Let's stay on track."

Another phone buzzed.

"Turn your phones off. Now," I said, raising my voice. "Enough!"

I resisted a desire to collect the phones because class was almost over. At the bell, I followed kids to the door, and Donnell, sweeping by my room, pulled me aside in the hall. "Get online!" she said. "There's been a school shooting in Newtown."

Flying over desks, I raced across the room to my phone. Newtown was where I lived, the town next-door to my school. Instantly, I tapped into the internet breaking news of the shooting, scrolling as fast as I could. I knew the school where it happened. Oh my God, I thought, we could be next. Our middle school—my classroom—was just six-and-a-half miles from Sandy Hook Elementary School in Newtown.

What I didn't know was that our principal had already put our school into a "perimeter lockdown": Students in portable classrooms behind the school had been escorted into computer labs in the main building for activities that teachers pretended had been planned. All ground-floor doors accessible from the outside were locked. No announcement was made over the loudspeaker. Teachers in far-flung upstairs rooms like mine had no inkling about this.

I silenced my phone and put it in my pocket as kids began arriving for the next class, my heart beating so hard I could barely concentrate on what I was saying. The news I had just read was too incomplete to share with my students, and I didn't want to invite questions I couldn't answer, questions I knew would only add to the uncertainty of the situation. There was a risk that someone in the class might blurt out a frightening half-truth and I wouldn't be able to counter it with solid assurances.

So I carried on, quietly saying goodbye to one student after another as they were called to the office for early dismissal. I noticed the remaining kids were now quieter. Clearly they were getting information. Finally, one boy couldn't help himself.

"Are we going to be shot?"

I froze, then answered instinctively.

"No. You are not. You are safe here," I said, trying to sound as reassuring as I could, though in reality I had very little confidence in my own words.

At the end of my last class, Mitchell, a lanky boy who rarely showed emotion, needed advice. What bus should he catch? Should he follow the plan for that day and take the one that dropped him off near his father's business not far from Sandy Hook Elementary School, or should he take the one to his mother's house even though she might not be home?

He borrowed my phone and left two voice messages.

"Dad, this is Mitch. I don't know where to come today."

"Mom, this is Mitch. Should I come to your house instead of

Dad's?"

Neither could respond before he had to go down to the buses and decide for himself. He chose his mother's house.

I wrote his words in my journal that night, rereading them now and then to remind myself what modern childhood had become.

After all the buses had left, teachers gathered in the library where we leaned on each other and on the long bookcases, dazed and crying. I was getting rapid-fire text messages from friends and my journalist husband, who had sped home from Manhattan to report the Newtown story for the Associated Press. A mentally disturbed 20-year-old had entered the school and shot and killed 20 first graders and six adult staff members before killing himself.

Other teachers were hearing from relatives and friends who had children at Sandy Hook Elementary, including one of our teachers, a friend, who had raced there to get her daughter—thankfully, unharmed. My friend returned to work a week later but only briefly before leaving for good, deciding to stay home for the sanity of her family.

Dave offered what details he could, saying no one knew for sure yet how many children had been hurt…or killed. Or how many staff members. He said more, but all I really remember is how he struggled to keep his voice level. Afterward, we fumbled our way to our cars, nine of us nervously driving toward Newtown, afraid to think about what we might find there.

Through tears, I saw the flag hanging at half-staff in front of our columned town hall. Main Street was quiet at first. Soon, though, people began to appear with armloads of bouquets which they laid gently in the courtyard of the building. Parents came with little children to drop off teddy bears with hearts and notes on them, tucking these among the bouquets.

As days passed, the collection grew, sprawling beneath hedges, on the grass, along the sides of the granite steps. From far away came more memorials. One school made thousands of origami swans that were hung inside the town hall, next to a row of tables containing boxes of sympathy cards from people all over the world. "We cry for you." "We wish you peace." The aftermath of the Sandy Hook shooting was a blur: peace vigils, tearful hugs among strangers, banners, television trucks with klieg lights. Around town bright yard displays for Christmas were unplugged. Then the town hall grounds and all those loving mementoes were covered with snow.

Not long afterward, construction began on the front of my own school building to create a bullet-proof vestibule between double doors, where visitors would be screened before they could enter. An armed safety officer joined our staff. Classroom door locks were replaced up and down the halls so that teachers could secure them from inside each room. Retractable shades were hung on all door windows.

A year later, when I asked my students to write about what they remembered of that terrible December day when a school shooting came so close to home, the kids didn't even pretend to open their journals. It was still too raw; too close. We needed a discussion instead. Morgan, a particularly honest girl, went first, saying that she didn't really trust anyone anymore.

"I don't think I'll ever be safe again," she said matter-of-factly. I stared at her long blonde bangs falling into dark eyes. She wasn't complaining, she was just stating a new fact of life: She was vulnerable—and she was on her own. I had heard that some Sandy Hook Elementary students who survived the shooting kept "weapons" under their pillows at night—table knives, screwdrivers, play swords. The terrible truth was, even at home, children no longer felt safe.

Mitchell, the boy who couldn't reach his parents by phone, told me how the shooting had changed his feelings about children. During the aftermath of the crisis, he had gone to his father's business in Sandy Hook and spent the Christmas holidays making deliveries to families that had lost a child.

"Now I notice little children," he said. "I worry about them."

And so, instead of writing in class, we talked about how we had been changed by that day.

For me, though I didn't say this out loud, nightmares regularly crowded my troubled sleep and jolted me awake with tears on my cheeks. Shooters stalked half-lit corridors as I scrambled futilely to lock my classroom door or dragged my heavy feet, slow motion, toward that door. The dream scenes changed from school-like settings to open parks or, once, a Victorian house where children milled in long hallways and I shouted to them to run for shelter—to what turned out to be an oversized bathroom with a clawfoot tub. The only constant in these fever dreams was my helplessness. I froze, I stumbled, I failed. In one nightmare, students and I sat frozen in the open, watching a bullet tear through the slit window of our door and then an arm shove through. Heart pounding, I woke up. If I was that rattled, I could only imagine how frightened my 12- and 13-year-old students must be.

"What if I'm in the bathroom?" One boy's voice pierced our class discussion. "What if I can't get back to the classroom before I'm locked out?"

Though we had been given talking points, there was no scripted answer for this question. I looked at him and said what I would have said to my son.

"Stay in the bathroom," I said, struggling to summon some kind of logic about what to say next. "Climb on top of the toilet. Make sure the door to the stall is locked. Be very quiet."

His eyes didn't leave my face. He wasn't satisfied.

"What if he comes into the bathroom?"

I took a breath and continued. "If someone comes into the bathroom and it looks empty, he will quickly move on."

Looking around the room, I saw that every face, every pair of eyes waited for more. What would I say next? "It's unlikely he will take the time to try to push open the door to a stall. For him, time is important. He wants to move into a place where there are lots of people. That's his goal."

What a thing to have to say. And yet all around, kids nodded. This message was not comforting, but it made sense.

After many shootings occurred around the country, every school developed protocols for emergency drills dictating behavior as soon as the unscheduled announcement from a loudspeaker cut the air:

"Attention: This is a lockdown drill."

Hearing it, students quickly and silently were to leave their desks and move to a designated area of the room or to a closet. As the teacher, I was to look into the hall for anyone who needed shelter before locking my door from the inside and then lowering the shade over the door's narrow window. Simultaneously, pre-assigned kids were to flip off light switches and close the blinds on our big window.

Then we would all sit soundlessly on the floor until a check of the building had been completed by our principal, assistant principals and our safety officer. Before it was over, the door handle of each room would rattle as one of them tried to open it. At those too-real moments, my eyes would flick from the students to the doorknob and back again. (During one drill my friend Anna, realizing in horror that she'd left her room key at home, tried to hold the doorknob still with her hands, until the principal jerked the door open. For an instant their eyes met, and later they had a sober chat in his office.)

After Sandy Hook, I became increasingly unhappy with the location of our designated gathering place—in front of the whiteboard. I understood that we needed to be away from the large wall of windows on the far side of the room and also away from the door. But that left us in the open, midway between door and windows.

I wanted the opposite: I wanted an invisibility cloak from which we could go "ninja" on any intruder, throwing chairs, phones, anything to survive. Talk about going off-script!

During one of our class discussions, I confessed I wasn't happy about the gathering spot.

"Let's get behind my desk, instead, even though it's by the windows," I said, explaining the unlikely threat of a second-floor assault through the windows. I spoke methodically, simply trying to sound practical.

After we pushed my large metal desk at an angle to create more room, all 23 kids practiced bunching behind it as quickly as they could. Having some defensive armor felt better to all of us. The desk became a shield, and we couldn't be seen from the door. When we practiced the change of location, it was clear that this kind of preparation had given most of us more courage. But we weren't there yet.

One boy looked at me in a way that said he had another idea. My glance encouraged him to share his plan.

"Let's put that long table in front of the door and the smaller table beside it at an angle. We could wedge them against the bookcase," he said, looking around at the other kids. "Then the door could never be forced open. Even if the locks were shot off."

Shot off. Those shocking words made me even more aware of the aching need for a sense of safety. I nodded. Immediately, he and another boy moved the tables into position and pushed against them. Nothing budged.

"Let's see how fast we can do it again," he suggested. This time a few other kids joined in to help, moving the tables back to their original positions and then shifting them into the protective wedge again—their movements wordlessly synchronized. The rest of us watched without a sound.

After everyone had returned to their desks, I wanted to say a few things. But I needed to control my surging emotions after witnessing this display of cooperation by my kids, this rehearsal of impromptu actions meant to save us all from an armed invader.

I began slowly. "I have learned that the most important part of my job is to protect you. I take that very seriously. I will do everything I can to see that you are not hurt." Though my eyes filled with tears, I noticed how intently kids watched my face without any sign of embarrassment. These were words they needed to hear, and words I needed to say. I was positive of that. "We are all together in this," I said.

What I had come to understand was that modern times demand a new pact between teachers and students. This commitment is so essential that learning can't take place until we have affirmed it out loud. When big-city terrorism becomes small-classroom terror, the very image of school has changed; school has become just another place to be rescued from. Teachers must be bold about that truth before moving on to vocabulary or algebra or any other lesson.

It occurred to me that our kids now face a whole new set of challenges that require, well, grit. That word again, defined by Webster as "firmness of mind or spirit, unyielding courage in the face of hardship or danger." It comes from within. I had watched my kids take initiative and wrestle heavy tables into wedges that would save us. They led the way. In so many respects, they had already stepped out from their childlike selves.

Today teachers must prepare our kids for a future that demands honesty and authenticity and requires us to stick together even as outside forces—a terrorist in a plane, a shooter in a school hallway, dark sites in technology's web, whatever—threaten to drive us apart.

# FIVE

# In the Trenches

My class was ready to dig into our first novel, which told the coming-of-age story of a middle-school boy whose little brother had leukemia. I was sure students would empathetically follow the tension and drama of this engaging story. I wasn't worried about the buy-in. What I faced was more complicated.

One of my students was battling leukemia in real life. Kyle, who missed most of sixth grade, was now in seventh grade and strong enough to attend school regularly. He would likely be in class as we opened our novel.

How could I offer up this invented drama to a boy who actually lived it, chemotherapy and all? How could I conduct class discussions with 12- and 13-year-olds who maybe knew—or, actually, almost certainly didn't know—that one of their number was fighting the same odds as the fictional boy they would come to care about in the book?

In *Drums, Girls, and Dangerous Pie*, author Jordan Sonnenblick's character Jeffrey had a better than 50 percent chance of beating acute lymphoblastic leukemia. I knew the real-world odds had improved since 2004, when the novel was written. But still.

This required delicate consideration. What were my options?

Number one: I could use a different book for Kyle's class. All of the coming-of-age books we read taught valuable lessons in addition to being exciting and sometimes funny. Young protagonists followed paths of self-discovery, learned the value of standing up for what they believed, found love in unusual places. I could dust off a perfectly good novel about a boy sent to an Alaskan island. There were lots of good angles here; kids could focus on Native Americans and forgiveness. It was a good book. But I didn't really want to switch.

Number two: I could plow through *Drums*, assuming Kyle wouldn't be in school that much and so would miss most discussion days. Maybe I was overthinking this. Besides, the boy with leukemia in the book was the younger brother, not the main character.

Number three: I could discuss the situation with Kyle's parents to explore how to involve him. I would need to see if they were comfortable with the prospect that Kyle might become a central focus as the class plunged into a fictional version of his reality. How would they receive that? Could I get them involved? Might they even come to class to support Kyle as we talked about the real-life effects of leukemia?

One night I turned to my journal, a habit I had acquired many decades before to get perspective on daily events. "We're in the trenches now," I wrote. Then, listing the options before me in longhand, I could feel a sharpening of focus. That allowed me to sleep comfortably that night.

Early the next day, after looking back over my words, I headed in to school. I decided to broach this intimate topic with the parents of a child I had not yet gotten to know. To prepare for the call, I wrote and rewrote my end of the conversation and finally summoned the composure I needed to pick up the phone. This was one of those times when I had to cross the line between the classroom and the living room of a student's family.

Kyle's mother, who I learned was a scientist, answered and I took a deep breath. "I'm Kyle's English teacher," I told her.

"Yes? Is everything okay."

"Everything's fine. I just wanted to talk to you about a novel we'll be reading that explores a situation I'm concerned about. One of the characters is a young boy who has leukemia."

She didn't say anything.

"He's not the main character," I continued, filling the silence. "But it seemed important to talk with you."

There was a pause, a long one, and then she spoke.

"We would like to see this novel," she said.

"Of course." I let out my breath. This time she filled the silence— saying she was glad I had contacted her, mentioning that she and her husband had discussed coming to the school to talk about Kyle's health with his teachers. "Maybe we could speak to your students as well."

As I sent the book home to Kyle's parents and imagined them discussing it, I felt an immense sense of relief. In the following days we emailed back and forth, and it seemed that something good might come out of an awkward and intrusive coincidence.

At the same time I enlisted the help of our seventh grade counselor, Michael, called "Mr. D" because no one could pronounce his last name.

While he finished a phone call, I sat on the sofa in his small office listening to the rhythmic chanting of his soft background music. One wall was covered by a large purple-and-yellow tie-dyed print. A small fountain on the windowsill gurgled away in the weak morning light. The faint scent of essence of geranium was almost pleasant. Michael swiveled toward me as he hung up and crossed one sandal-clad foot over the other. He had told me once that he would never cut his hair again (for a reason I've forgotten), and true to his promise, it continued to grow past his shoulders.

I told him that Kyle, the boy with leukemia, was in my class and I handed him a copy of *Drums*, briefly explaining the plot and the leukemia-stricken character. "I've contacted Kyle's parents and sent them a copy of the book," I said, "but I just wanted to know if you'd be willing to participate in a class discussion, if need be. Maybe help smooth the way."

"Hmm," he said, turning the book over to scan the back cover. "Let's see if we can do something positive with this."

His phone rang and he let it take a message. I liked Michael a lot. He was always eager to come into class, but sometimes his approach was unorthodox. I knew I needed to stay in touch with him and on top of things. I also needed to directly address the person at the center of this.

When Kyle next showed up in class, wearing a heavy coat with a hood and pulling his books in a rolling cart, his sweet face was quick to smile. I took the plunge. Standing quietly in the corner of the room, I said, "As I think you may know, we are going to be reading a book about a character with leukemia. Did your parents mention this to you?"

Kyle nodded.

"Did they show you the book I sent home?"

He nodded.

"How do you feel about being in class while we read this book?"

Kyle murmured something I couldn't quite hear, then said, "It's okay." His shrug suggested he saw few options. A decision had been made. But was that really what he felt, or was it just my impression?

As we prepared to start the book, the situation remained a bit murky, and it was further complicated by the news that Kyle's parents, both very busy, would not be able to schedule a visit. I returned to Michael's office, next door.

"Help."

Michael swiveled toward me.

"Kyle's parents can't come in. How can I set the stage for this novel?" I felt an edge of panic creep into my voice.

"Let me think about this," Michael said.

I was not reassured. It was Tuesday, and I needed to hand out the books the following Monday, coordinating lessons with Shannon, the English teacher of the other half of the seventh grade. On Friday, I asked Michael if he could sit down with me and Kyle at lunchtime to figure out a plan for launching the novel.

The three of us gathered in his office, Kyle twirling half circles in the swivel chair, Michael sitting comfortably cross-legged opposite me on the second sofa. They looked at each other, and Michael spoke.

"Kyle and I have been talking. We've decided to have a dialogue, sort of a question-and-answer between the two of us for the other kids to witness."

My startled expression must have revealed my confusion.

"Let's show her," Kyle said, his grin broadening to show perfect white teeth. They each pulled out a script. It turned out they'd been rehearsing in secret.

"When did you learn you had leukemia, Kyle?" the counselor asked in such a gentle voice that I caught my breath. Kyle answered in soft but clear words, looking intently at Mr. D.

"Describe how you found out." Again, Kyle spoke without faltering, offering details and explanations of his struggle. This back-and-forth continued for a few minutes; the effect of their exchange was heart-stopping for me.

"Wow," I said, finally exhaling. I wanted to hug both of them.

Over the weekend, I became convinced the whole seventh grade needed to hear this classmate's story. I emailed Shannon and we arranged to combine our classes for the presentation. That meant that each of the five classes throughout the day would double in size as they met together in one room. That's when I started to worry again. Would that large crowd be too much for Kyle? Would he have the stamina to make it through five classes in one day? What if he faltered?

Other questions nagged: How would the audience, a packed room of seventh graders, behave? I knew that sometimes when kids felt awkward they laughed or blurted out hurtful words to cover their own feelings. How would they respond to a boy most knew very little about? How could I protect Kyle from the potential insensitivity of the wise guys? No answers came.

Finally I told myself, yes, it would be a risky encounter, but I had to bank on past experience, which taught me that authentic emotional exchanges were worth the risk. When we are honest with children, a protective shield comes over us all.

On Monday morning, kids clumped into the first class, and joyful chatter broke out when they noticed the announcement on the board that we were moving to join the class across the hall for a special presentation. I explained that a fellow student would be talking about a life challenge and Mr. D would moderate. I reminded them how important it was to be respectful. And I tried to project a look that said there would be hell to pay if they weren't.

Though they tried to be quiet, my students were bubbling as we crossed the hall to a room that already contained 23 kids, including friends. They found places in extra chairs, and on counters at the back; some shared the window ledge.

Up front were two swivel chairs. Kyle was wearing his coat and holding a microphone. At first, he appeared to be very small. I patted him on the shoulder and then went to the side of the room near the door. Once everyone was settled, Michael held up his microphone and opened the presentation by introducing Kyle just as if he was a 40-year-old colleague. Then, as he had done in the rehearsal for me, he began: "Kyle, when did you first learn you had leukemia?"

Kyle almost whispered his answer. Mr. D gestured for him to move the microphone closer.

"When I was in fifth grade," he repeated, peering over his coat collar.

I pulled my eyes away from Kyle's face to check the reactions of the other students. There was no finger tapping. No playing with hair. All eyes were fixed on him.

"Can you explain to us what leukemia is?"

Kyle's voice got stronger. He spoke into the mic with more authority. His face emerged above his collar as he turned toward the audience.

"Well," he said, "leukemia is a condition where there is an abnormal number of white blood cells in the blood. It causes easy bruising, and bleeding. And it makes me tired."

He sounded like a cross between a textbook and a professor. His audience barely breathed.

"How do you treat leukemia?"

Kyle looked at Michael, then at the class.

"I get chemotherapy. That's a drug that kills the bad cells. Now I have a port in my chest. It's like a small opening so the doctor doesn't have to put a needle in my veins every four weeks to give me the drug."

I looked around again. Some heads were shaking. Eyes widened. Hannah's hand covered her mouth.

"What are some of the hardest times for you?" Mr. D asked.

"Well..." This time, Kyle's voice grew sadder and quieter. We had to lean in to pick up his words.

"I have to be in the hospital a lot. I can't be with other kids that much. And it was really bad in sixth grade when my two younger brothers had to be sent to live with our grandparents. My parents needed to concentrate on me. We had to be sure I didn't get any germs," he said, looking at his lap. "I missed my brothers."

Some kids wiped their eyes.

"What about some of the happiest times?" the counselor asked.

Kyle lifted his head, looked out at the large group and beamed. His words tumbled out. "Each summer we get to go to this great camp, and now even my brothers go. It's for kids who have leukemia."

Around the room shoulders relaxed at the news that Kyle's brothers were back.

"We get to swim and go on boats and have bonfires and great food. I have so much fun at this camp. My whole family loves it." As he talked, Kyle smiled into the eyes of his fellow seventh graders.

"You can volunteer at this camp if you'd like," he said.

Hannah raised the hand that had covered her mouth. "Do you have a website?" He recited it and added, "It's really fun."

Checking the clock, the counselor spoke. "Well, it's just about time for us to wrap up our interview, Kyle. I have one last question." He paused briefly.

"What are you grateful for?"

Grateful: The notion seemed incongruous. Some kids squirmed while others looked at each other, then down at their desks or hands.

Kyle didn't hesitate.

"I'm grateful for my parents who take care of me."

Now I didn't dare look out at the other kids for fear of crying myself.

"I'm grateful that I can come to school this year more than I could last year."

He concluded simply, "I'm grateful that I am stronger."

Mr. D offered a full smile to Kyle. "Thank you so much for sharing your experience with us," he said. "We have all learned a lot."

The kids stood and applauded. Kyle was taken aback. He nodded, locking eyes with Mr. D as if he was hanging onto an anchor in a swelling tide. The bell rang.

I studied the kids as they filed out. Instead of the usual chattering with each other, they were quiet, turned inward, some grabbing tissues from a box by the door. They had come in worrying about who they would sit next to at lunch. They left feeling grateful to be alive.

Amir lingered behind. This tough kid, just back from a suspension for fighting on the bus, walked slowly to the front of the room, hands in the pockets of his black hoodie.

I moved forward nervously. He was unpredictable, but I knew he was beginning to show some vulnerability. Now he sometimes revealed in his journal details about the battles he faced at home and the insults that came his way at school. There was another thing I knew: He had asked me to help him write a Facebook post, a thank-you to his mother. As he approached Kyle, he looked as if he had met someone new, someone who might understand him.

"Hey thanks, man," Amir's gravelly voice said, holding the stare. Dark eyes met dark eyes. Kyle's experience with the world had schooled him in pain and fear. He greeted the stranger with tenderness—and a fist bump.

"No problem," Kyle said softly. Amir turned to follow the others out.

I stopped at Michael's office at the end of the day and fell onto the sofa. "You. Are. Amazing," I said.

"I know, I know," he said, smiling broadly. I hugged him.

That night, I went over and over Kyle's words as I was falling asleep. His job was to get well, but he had no power to make that happen. His essential message to us was he didn't have time for petty thoughts. His agenda was clear. A storm had come through and blown away all the litter of his life. He was left with just one shiny hope.

The next day, I decided we would write in our journals and then talk about how we had been affected. If Kyle came to class, we would be able to say these things right in front of him.

But something else happened before I could assign the journal writing. Hannah asked to speak to me. I guessed it might be about the sharp, new braces that were clearly pricking her lips, but, no, she said she had been up late the night before, thinking. She asked if she could read a poem she had written about her parents' divorce.

I paused. Kids were generally reluctant to read personal poems until we knew each other better. My guess was that Kyle's presentation had cracked open some emotional lockbox. I wanted to protect her from what might have been a seventh grader's impulse.

Privately I asked her, "Are you sure you want to open yourself up in front of the whole class?"

"Yes," she said, locking me in her steady blue gaze, not backing down. I asked to read the poem first.

As kids came into the room, I tuned out the sound of their chatter and dropping of books on desks, and read the poem. It was written straight from a 13-year-old's heart, and I caught my breath. If she was going to read this out loud, I warned her, she couldn't take it back.

"I've thought about that," she said. "My friends already know all about it, and I feel okay about sharing with the other kids. They'll understand."

I swept the class, looking at kids' faces, finally settling on Mac, who had a unique ability to disrupt whatever the plan was. I didn't trust him to behave himself during this reading. He might interrupt with ridiculously loud finger-popping, a fake cough, or by endlessly flipping his pencil up in the air. He might blurt another of his endless requests to go to the nurse. Or worse, say something mocking.

Now I would just have to cross my fingers that the gravity of Hannah's poem might silence him. As soon as everyone was seated, I went to the front of the room and caught their eyes, pausing to zero in on Mac.

"We have a guest speaker today," I said. This, as always, prompted a happy hum and a buzz.

"Hannah has asked if she can share a personal poem she's written about her parents' divorce. This is a brave act on her part and quite a privilege for us. I don't need to tell you how respectfully we must handle this gift."

Hannah came forward to sit on a stool at the front, a soft blush lighting her face. She looked right out at the other students and started.

She spoke of "2 nations at war" creating "2 houses to stay at," leaving her with "2 halves of a heart."

When she finished no one moved. I risked a quick glance at Mac. He was expressionless. Hannah slipped off the stool, holding her paper, and looked back at me. No one wanted to pierce the painful intimacy that seemed to hold us all.

As she moved back toward her desk, someone started clapping and soon the whole class joined in. "That was awesome!" "Wow!" They expressed their admiration in a seventh-grader's way.

By sharing her burden, Hannah had connected us. We valued that. Our burdens varied, but in fact the dual living situation caused by divorce was commonplace. Teachers often had to anticipate the organizational challenge when a student said she had stayed at her mother's house while her homework or her book was at her father's. We even gave some kids two sets of books and set up separate hotlines to the father and mother.

One boy, chronically missing homework, used the split home as his explanation for months—until we learned his parents lived only two blocks apart; he could easily walk between the two.

"Guess I can't use that line again," he said sheepishly.

"No," Donnell told him. "You've been busted."

But for Hannah to explore the pain of divorce, not just the inconvenience of it, was a new thing. It was in the midst of this reflection that Mac raised his hand to go to the nurse.

What this time? I thought. A loose tooth? A concussion? A spontaneous broken leg? "What is it, Mac?"

"Headache."

"Here," I said, holding out a pass. And out he went.

Meanwhile, other kids began writing in their journals about the new perspectives they had gained while listening to Kyle's story.

In different words, many repeated the same message: They were moved by hearing him talk so bravely about the needles and the pain and missing his brothers.

"I feel stupid complaining about school when Kyle said he was grateful to be strong enough to come to school," wrote one.

Another: "I never knew anyone like that. I never knew anyone who might die."

In my newsletter to parents at the end of the *Drums* unit, I wrote, "We took our novel to greater heights with the powerful insight of a classmate who was interviewed by Mr. D about his own fight with leukemia. His presentation was transformative. And it led to a brand new assignment—writing imaginative narratives about how struggles can shape each of us."

I especially remember the narratives of one boy and one girl.

The boy told about his handicapped sister and brother: One who couldn't speak and the other so emotionally disturbed that any trip out in public could end in ranting rages. Exploring his hard-earned love for his siblings, he wrote: "I guess I see the world very differently from my friends. But that's okay because some things that are hard for others aren't as hard for me."

The girl told about her father's debilitating depression and how she had learned to read his moods and take advantage of his good days: "I see little kids in the park with their fathers pushing them on the swings. I never had that. But I love my father and I know he is doing the best he can."

That night I opened my own journal and wrote about all that had happened. I thought about the intimacy students and teachers share as a year unfolds, especially as we feel the underground rumblings of the volcano we call seventh grade.

A school year is not just about time passing, not just about academic lessons learned and tests taken. It's about being in the trenches. It's about courage and honesty. It's about reassuring each other that we are not alone. And when that happens, it's about doing what Amir did with Kyle—simply saying thank you.

# SIX

# Belonging

When Chenlee was steered into my classroom by another Chinese-speaking student, I was surprised by how tall and willowy she was compared to her petite guide. Perhaps her height was exaggerated by a graceful neck and hair expertly pinned on top of her head.

Luckily, Deborah had prepped me on this new student who was also assigned to her remedial reading class. Chenlee couldn't speak a word of English and had recently arrived from a children's home in China to join an American family.

Much of her childhood had been spent as the oldest girl in the orphanage, mothering the babies as they were dropped off until, one by one, they were taken into families, leaving her behind. She had known disappointment and would express gratitude toward her own adoptive family often: first in simple drawings with hearts and smiles, then in words, sentences and paragraphs as she doggedly pushed herself to overcome the newness and strangeness of English. If we were all driven to find a common language in this class, none was more so than Chenlee.

So there we were, facing each other across her neat pile of notebooks crowned by a dazzling purple pencil case. Our school had too few non-English-speaking students at that time to warrant a special program. Our training called for us to "scaffold" assignments according to students' ability. This could mean setting these newcomers up in a corner desk with a laptop translation program where they could peck away at vocabulary. I knew what that kind of lonely felt like. So, rather than an isolating laptop experience, I chose an approach that was messier but I thought more valuable. It would include foreign-language speakers—and to some extent all challenged learners—in the warmth of the circle of other kids, even if the words they heard were unintelligible at first. My natural trust in immersion usually paid off.

These out-of-place kids needed friends to share a new language with; formal instruction would come later. Wouldn't the lesson of inclusion bear dividends for the English speakers too, at least those who could imagine finding themselves in a strange place some day, alone and different, as I had been when transplanted from Georgia to New York? They needed to learn how to reach out. They needed to be something like a family. Looking around the room, that's what I wanted to see: something like siblings helping each other.

I made it clear to the class, that, thanks to Chenlee, we all had a rare opportunity to learn about a new country, new customs, some words from a new language. After the first few weeks, I'd always ask any new non-English-speaking student to write a word or two in their language on the white board so we could practice pronunciation. Our stumbling efforts—mine first, of course—made everyone laugh, especially the new student. One day, Chenlee read aloud an excerpt from the then-popular vampire novel, *Twilight*—in Mandarin. We swooned at the sounds and marveled at page after page of indecipherable pictograph characters as she passed the book around and glowed in the spotlight.

On Chenlee's first day, she had handed me an intricately folded paper bracelet and her long, slender fingers maneuvered it onto my wrist. No words needed to be said.

In another class, it was another language. Carlos D. and Carlos B., both new, had arrived a few weeks apart from different parts of Brazil. I asked one Carlos, who knew a little English, "Do you know any poetry in Portuguese that you can recite?" He translated to the other Carlos, and they instantly began trading phrases back and forth. Titles? Lines of verse? I wasn't sure what was going on. Then, in perfect unison, they recited the same poem! Without understanding a single word, the other kids embraced this magical communication.

"How'd you do that?" someone asked. The question was clearly a compliment.

Even as I embraced the chaos that receiving a non-English-speaking student represented, there was another kind of chaos that I certainly did not embrace and in fact hated.

A perfect example of that came on the same day that Chenlee had given me the paper bracelet; it involved the hard-headed Cameron, who regularly challenged my grading. His argument this time involved points lost on essay questions that explored the novel we had just finished. I was reviewing for the class a set of exemplary responses. All my students knew this was not the time for individual quibbles; those conversations happened privately. But, Cameron raised his hand, pretending he had a general question. What he really wanted was a brawl.

As the class listened and as I tried to divert him, Cameron loudly read one of his answers and challenged the notations I'd made in the margin. He assured us all that his friends agreed with him. This kind of brinksmanship can produce an exciting verbal altercation between teacher and student. Maybe the teacher would lose her temper. Maybe the student would win this round. The entire class was ringside, eager for the bout.

"Not now, Cameron. Let's move on," I said.

He persisted until I resorted to verbal jujitsu.

"Okay, Cameron, meet me for lunch. We'll discuss this then."

The class was disappointed to see the sparring end. As for Cameron, he considered it a tie, maybe even worth sacrificing his lunch.

When the clock registered lunchtime, I quickly grabbed a bottle of water from my refrigerator, hoping I might get a quick sip and a bite of my sandwich before he arrived. That's when a movement caught my eye and I looked up to see not Cameron, but Logan, trudging through the door, shoulders slumped, wavy hair hanging in his face.

"You're not going to lunch?" I asked him.

Sliding his locker open and pulling out a lumpy paper bag, he said, "I don't have any friends."

Pause.

I was tempted to contradict him with reassurances. His expression was bland, his voice emotionless, his words almost a dare. But I knew better. I had been schooled against falsely propping up the egos of adolescents by the story told in a young-adult novel sent to me by my teacher-sister, Laurie. *Eleanor and Park*, the sometimes raw but riveting tale of two high schoolers living on the fringe, had prepared me. When Eleanor used Logan's same words, "I don't have any friends," she was not feeling sorry for herself. She was simply stating the fact of her life as an outsider. She was different and she knew it. Besides, she didn't really consider the kids at her school worthy or even capable of understanding her.

Logan lived the life of an outsider. Like Eleanor, he had little in common with other students. Rescued by his grandparents from a drug-addicted mother, he had experienced plenty of disillusionment, especially when it came to his long-absent father. He had no siblings. Without any semblance of a conventional life to draw on, Logan coexisted with his classmates by playing the wild boy. Hair down to his shoulders, he wore the same black sweatpants and red hoodie each day. He resisted reading, classwork, homework.

But inside his head, thoughts were whirring. Logan loved to watch science channels and memorized TV documentaries. Facts about the eyesight of cats or the temperature at which clay becomes ceramic would tumble from his lips. He proved to us that bears don't hibernate.

As he stood there holding his lunch bag, I refused to say anything dishonest about his "no friends" comment. "Logan," I finally said, "yes, you are yourself, not like everybody else. But you know kids like having you around. Take David. I see you guys laughing all the time."

After a second of looking at me, he agreed: "Yeah, we do have the same sense of humor." I wasn't sure where this was going, but at that point he suddenly turned to leave, glancing into his lunch bag. "I hope my grandma packed grapes."

I watched him nudge himself down the hall, and realized for the hundredth time how important it was for kids to see a larger picture. The petri dish of the classroom was only one version of belonging. Logan's connection to the universe was a bit tenuous, almost invisible. But whether he saw it or not, he was part of the web. We all were.

Just then, turning at the top of the stairs and moving like a heat-seeking missile toward me, came Cameron. Shoulders set. As he got closer, I could see the resolve in his eyes—which were beady in the best of times and were absolutely piercing at the moment. I braced myself.

Without hesitating, Cameron produced his test and pointed to one of my written comments.

"This is pointless," he said.

I shook my head at his insolent tone, but kept my expression as neutral as I could. Remember how I said I have a tendency to swear at times? At that moment my thoughts shouted, "B.S.!" Aloud, I said, "Bad start."

"Sorry," he said, then countered, "But why did you write this question? You know the answer." He rolled his eyes.

"Of course," I said. "But your response is not complete unless you explain the text instead of just repeating it."

His interrogation continued, point-by-point. I played possum, letting him storm, because I knew he might soon tire and thus be more willing to listen. After a while, I spoke up. "One important difference between a really good paper, and a, well"—I paused an extra beat—"a mediocre paper is the inclusion of detail." In class, I had stressed this point ad nauseam. "Text support" might be teacher talk, but it really makes a difference.

By the time we finished dissecting my margin comments, we came to a startling new discovery: I had miscalculated the number of points off. Cameron's grade should have been lower; not a B, but a B-minus!

Now seeing that he hadn't won any points back and might even lose more, he melted. Those defiant, piercing eyes softened almost into tears. Something came over me.

"I won't take those other points off," I said. "And I'm sure you'll nail it next time." This—plus a compliment on some of his well-chosen words—left him somewhat encouraged.

The trouble was I knew it wouldn't stand up at home because his parents insisted on nothing less than straight A's. Cameron mumbled something conciliatory and pushed back his chair. Here was the wounded soldier wondering how he was going to tell the general he had not taken the hill.

I watched him leave, forgetting for a minute I had missed my own lunch. At least I would have time for a few grapes. Bright leaves had almost finished falling from the trees outside the classroom window. The sky was a dome of vivid blue. The heating unit rumbled and clanked into action.

How were Chenlee, Logan and Cameron all connected in this seventh-grade universe? That is what we all needed to learn. Science class tells us that matter is connected. Social studies tells us that events are connected. Math shows us how to connect numbers or points on a line. In English class we learn how people—their lives, their troubles, their hopes —are connected. Literature helps us understand how we belong, and it also lets us try on different experiences of belonging; it allows us to experiment without risk, to learn through the actions of others, to practice becoming whole human beings.

A brief short story, just two-and-a-half pages, that we started reading the following week made this so clear. It was Langston Hughes' "Thank You, M'am." First published in the late 1950s, the story tells about Roger, a skinny kid not much older than my students, who tries to steal a purse from an older woman on the streets of Harlem. The strap breaks and she grabs him by the scruff of his neck, delivers a loud lecture and marches him to her apartment. At some point he stops trying to escape, though he has chances. The woman orders him to wash his face while she fixes dinner.

"You ought to be my son. I could teach you right from wrong," she tells him. The words echoed around the room as I read the story aloud.

At her small table the two talk. Louella Bates Washington Jones tells Roger that her life has not been easy. After dinner, she hands him the ten dollars he admits he was trying to get from her pocketbook. He says he wanted a pair of blue suede shoes. Next time, she tells him, don't steal. You could have asked. Behave yourself. As he leaves he tries to thank her, but she has already closed the door.

We finished the story. Our classroom was a world of silence and furrowed brows. None of the expected outcomes had materialized. To analyze this story, we had to start upstream, seeking inferences that would help us understand what had just happened.

A boy, probably poor, maybe homeless, tried to steal a pocketbook. His victim, a woman, showed him what we agreed was "tough love" and shared a meal and her money with him. The story had little dialogue and few direct clues as to cause and effect. So, we had to work on indirect ones. Let's talk, I suggested.

"Why didn't she call the police?" This was Cameron, always the first to comment. "That's what she should have done."

Hailey, managing to get through the day without her phone (which had been confiscated in math class), asked, "Why didn't he try harder to get away?'"

This tale was something of a photo negative: What didn't happen told the story as thoroughly as what did. Mrs. Jones didn't call the police. Roger didn't try to run after he got to the apartment. But, I wasn't going to tell the class. I was going to ask questions.

"What was this story really about? Was Roger changed by this un-expected experience?" Roughly half the class responded no, heads shaking.

"Oh, I think he was changed," said Bronwyn softly. She brought the same penetrating eye to this story that she had used to understand the buttoned-up anger of Amir.

Cameron looked at her, head tilting, almost frowning. I knew Bronwyn saw exactly how this fictional character, this discarded boy, had been touched by the kindness of the woman he had tried to rob, because Bronwyn had also been touched by it. She had been changed herself and so she interpreted Roger's feelings using her own. Beyond that, she was able to peer into the heart of Mrs. Jones.

"How do you know he changed?" I asked Bronwyn. She and the other students analyzed the characters' actions, using every shred of evidence—their clothing, facial expressions, words, gestures—to draw their conclusions. According to the narrator, Mrs. Jones avoided asking questions about the boy's home life so as not to embarrass him. Here we had to consider what she didn't do: She didn't pry.

Instead, Mrs. Jones described her job at a hairdresser's shop and ac-knowledged that she had also wanted things she couldn't have when she was young. She added that she'd done things she wouldn't tell him. At the end she hurried him out. The door closed, and the story concluded, "He never saw her again."

We swam back up to the class discussion, and I tried to find a more pointed question: "What did this boy think when the lady told him to use the warm water in the sink to wash his face and then handed him a clean towel and told him to comb his hair?"

Bronwyn spoke first: "That was so kind. So respectful. It reminded me of her words, 'You should have been my son.' In a way, for a moment, he was her son."

Others murmured and looked at each other. Almost speaking to himself, Logan mused, "I guess at that moment he didn't really want to run away."

I thought about the rescue in Logan's own life, the offer from his grandparents to take him in. It was not the traditional order of things, but didn't everyone need to be cared for? Perhaps reading this fictional story helped him understand his own real-life story.

I looked over the class and asked, "What actually happened when they sat down and shared lima beans, ham and hot cocoa?" My question apparently touched a nerve in Seth, who responded, "It seemed like at that moment he was part of a family. Food can do that. It's like Mrs. Jones showed him so much by her actions. She didn't tell him as much as she showed him."

No one in class knew better than Seth about empty words. He'd given up on most adults in his life because they were all talk and no action. More and more he turned to smoking marijuana on the roof of his house. It had taken me a month to show him I took him seriously.

Things were happening in the classroom in front of me: Logan feeling less abandoned, Seth not feeling so let down, Bronwyn optimistically trusting human nature. They were taking in more than a fictional, accidental meeting of strangers. Through a few pages of resonant fiction, they were able to see this meeting for what it was, a small miracle.

"Will Roger ever steal again?" I asked.

Bronwyn and Logan shook their heads. "Never," she said, solemnly. "Probably not," he said.

"Why not?" I asked, looking around.

Hailey spoke up. After all, this was about a relationship. "Because, for the first time, he knew someone out there cared," she said.

Cameron, perhaps glimpsing something beyond a mere grade, added, "Maybe he felt like he mattered."

I looked at him with unexpected fondness. Maybe that's what Cameron wanted more than anything—to matter. His constant struggle for a better grade might be part of a campaign to prove that he counted.

Then, another voice: "And for once he was not alone." It was the sad, tough Amir, who was always alone.

I had to wonder as these students checked in, seeming to match their own lives against the fictional scenario. Did they hear each other's confiding words the same way I did?

Now Patricia, the invisible girl, joined in. "He got respect for the first time," she said, "with food and a clean towel and warm water."

"Yes, yes, yes," I blurted. Quickly realizing I needed to restrain my exuberance. Respect was something Patricia had felt deprived of, as far as I could tell. I also wondered if she felt included today as she identified with Roger. As he was emotionally embraced by the students, perhaps she also felt embraced.

Seth picked up where he had left off before: "He knows he can be a better person."

"Yes!" I almost shouted before reeling myself in. Could this be the beginning of a similar lesson for Seth? When Mrs. Jones showed Roger she believed in him, Roger knew he could change. He could become the boy Mrs. Jones wanted to admire. Could Seth do that for his parents, for his teachers?

I glanced at the clock. We still had a little more time. "Why did she give him the money?" I asked. "What was her goal or motivation?"

A new speaker, Mae, the pianist, jumped in. She was great with musical notes but tone-deaf in this discussion. A literalist, struggling with inferential thinking (I was working with her on this), she took a wrong turn.

"She shouldn't have done that," Mae said. "It's the wrong message. He'll think the plan worked. 'Try to steal and someone will give you money.' That was not smart of her," Mae said.

I bit my tongue, saying nothing. Amir spoke up again, turning toward the class from his seat in the front.

"No. You don't get it," he said, a little brusquely. "She's showing him there are people in the world who understand his situation." I wondered if doing the puzzle with Amir had helped him realize that I understood his situation.

My turn again: "Why does she want to help Roger?"

The class energy level was still high. Kids' answers burst forth like popcorn. Nobody bothered to raise hands.

"Maybe she was like him when she was young and somebody helped her," said Bronwyn.

"Or, maybe," Amir countered, "she was like Roger but nobody helped her."

"Mrs. Jones could see it was a turning point for him," Seth added. "If she helped him, he could change."

Amir again: "Or, if she didn't help it would be too late because he had no one else."

Time for me to play devil's advocate.

"Wait, they're strangers, aren't they? She doesn't have any responsibility for him, does she?"

Instant responses: "Yes!"

One beat later, just a little quieter: "No!"

The contradictions were fascinating to explore. Some students were certain Mrs. Jones had to act because all humans owe that to each other. Others said she owed him nothing; they were not related, not really connected. Once we arrived at this philosophical crossroads, we could take up the larger issue of personal responsibility in society.

I sensed a need for a breather. "Turn to the person next to you," I said, "and talk a little more, privately, about some of these new ideas and focus on this one question: In general, do people have any fundamental obligation toward each other?"

I wandered the room overhearing conversations. Patricia told her partner this all reminded her of the "pay it forward" commercial on TV in which strangers intercepted falling objects before they struck another person, retrieved a baby's dropped toy, or simply held open a door. What goes around comes around.

Some kids' positions reflected a personal slant. Mae proclaimed firmly to Hailey: "I'm only responsible for my little brother and my dog. Nothing else."

Hailey didn't argue but said, "My mother and I were trying to find baking soda for a science experiment the other night, and I panicked because the store didn't have it. Then out of the blue, this nice lady who had overheard us tapped my mother on the shoulder and told her there was some at the Dollar Store right next door. She had no reason to help us except to be nice. We were really just strangers."

Mae came right back: "That's different. You were with your mother. I'd get in trouble if I just started talking to a stranger. It could be dangerous."

Seth broke away from his partner to join this exchange: "Sure, you don't talk to some bum or dangerous-looking guy. But if you could help someone, wouldn't you do it? Think about it; you do it for others because you want them to do it for you when your time comes."

Was this Seth? I made a quick mental note to share his awakening, or whatever was going on here, with the other teachers. Some, particularly Donnell, were hell-bent on putting Seth on a "behavior plan," which would result in consequences each time he failed to do homework or classwork, or committed any of a number of technical infractions. His daily actions would be recorded on a chart that he'd have to carry around for each teacher to sign. Besides being humiliating, the chart would probably disappear on the first day. And then where would we be?

There was just enough time for me to lob one last question to the whole class. "What if no one helped anyone?" I waited a long moment. "What kind of a world would we live in?"

Kids pictured the scene: Patricia's "pay it forward" commercial gone awry, the falling object striking the pedestrian. Several students murmured almost at once: "Terrible."

Class was almost over. I tapped my podium. "It's one thing to think about how one individual should or could act, but it's important to multiply that behavior and imagine a whole society of people acting like that. When Seth said, 'you do it for others because you would want it done for you,' he's talking about a world in which people look out for each other. Let's hold that thought as we leave class. And let's remember it when we're in class." I couldn't help adding: "Great thinking today. By all of you. Bravo!"

Kids gathered their books, remarking on the story or each other's comments. Because I had quoted Seth, someone teasingly said: "Oh, let me give tribute to the great mind of Seth." He responded with a slow half-smile, as he tossed his hair off his forehead.

I remembered once giving an easy journal writing assignment before I had gotten to know Seth: "Write about an event in your life worth remembering."

Seth had stretched his long khaki-clad legs out into the aisle, crossed his ankles above the loafers (no socks) and leaned back in his chair. As if from above, he watched other students scribbling away like so many ants. Clearly he viewed the assignment as unworthy. When I stopped by his desk he said, simply, "I can't think of anything." There was that half-smile again.

We talked for a minute and then I said quietly, "You can sketch a character if you like."

After a moment, Seth picked up his pencil. "I know," he said. "I'll write about when my little brother was born." There was a flash of mischievous merriment in his eyes.

When I checked his journal after school, I was surprised to see the word "hate"—used once, twice, three times. This was a story of a sibling's birth?

"I hated my stepfather," he wrote, "and even more I hated my mother for divorcing my father. The news of the baby did nothing but confirm my feelings for them all."

His grandfather talked him into going to the hospital. "He told me I was important to my little brother." At the hospital he still had to be persuaded to go in and see the baby.

"When I picked up my little brother, everything changed," he wrote, then finished with this line: "And now, five years later, whenever I think about hating my mother and stepfather, I think of my brother and I forgive them all."

I went back to the beginning to that repeated word "hate." If Seth had used this to shock me, as with that kid in summer school who wrote about finding her mother's boyfriend hanged, I wasn't upset. I welcomed truth, even when it was untidy. Rather than shocking me it showed me he wanted to belong.

Again I thought of the class as a family—a metaphor that quickly prompted a memory of my actual family. My mother had a tart comeback whenever one of her five children resisted reasonable directions and behaved badly: "Join the human race," she'd say.

# SEVEN

# Reading Dickens

They were all crowded at the big window. "Is it sticking? Will it be early dismissal?"

Even the slightest swirl of snowflakes glimpsed through the classroom window triggered a distraction—more so as the Christmas holidays approached.

Out in the hallway we heard music. The band teacher was guiding a group of young musicians toward our corner of the building, playing a medley: "Jingle Bells," "Deck the Halls," "Santa Claus is Coming to Town."

With each new class, boys and girls delivered gifts to me: homemade cookies in cellophane, mugs filled with Italian chocolates wrapped in gold and silver foil, candles, gift cards in bright envelopes.

"You can open it right now," they'd say hopefully.

Over the years I've received memorable presents: a blown glass pen with metal nib and a bottle of ink, a delicate Christmas ornament made from a dried starfish, and one rarity, a nice bottle of wine from a family that had just moved from Italy and hadn't yet picked up on American puritanism. I tucked it behind my laptop. When my friend Libby joined a group of us for lunch at the round table in my room, she asked in astonishment, "You got a bottle of wine? That kid gets an A!"

Oh yes. I looked forward to sipping that Valpolicella while working on my own Christmas menu later that week. Again I'd make my mother's tomato aspic recipe and there would be 15 twice-baked potatoes and casseroles and, of course, turkey.

In the hubbub before class started, kids shared information about fun activities happening in other classes, making sure they spoke loud enough for me to hear.

"There's a party in social studies."

"We played a game in math."

"The other literacy class is watching *Mulan!*"

Our class would not be watching a Disney movie. I had my own plan for preventing all structure from being swept away in the pre-vacation tidal wave, though I knew the kids wouldn't like it at first.

"We are going to read aloud and act," I announced. "We are going to bring on…Charles Dickens."

"Nooooooo," they groaned in unison. Then, one after another: "Why don't we play hangman?"

"Seven-up?"

"Four corners?"

"Can't we listen to music?"

In a way they were right; there were a thousand other ways to spend this edge-of-holiday time. With a pang, I remembered an experiment I had once tried at this time of year. It was inspired by a casual class conversation that had continued to bother me at the end of the day. A girl in my homeroom gushed that she used to love Christmas. "I couldn't wait to come downstairs that morning to see what was under the tree. I was always surprised."

Then in a voice drained of spirit, she continued: "Now, my mom just gives me her credit card and a spending limit, and I buy my own presents. I even wrap them." She looked sad and so did the other students. That thrill associated with her childhood had evaporated and along with it the expectancy and emotion that come with receiving a gift.

What is a gift? I thought. What makes it special? This was a worthy reflection, especially at this time of year, I thought. I wanted to offer my kids a reassuring message; something deeper about the nature of gift-giving.

I remembered something I'd read in an issue of the monthly magazine our middle school subscribed to as a resource for fiction and nonfiction reading. It was an excerpt from *The Glass Castle*, an edgy memoir I had read in full a few years earlier, about the gypsy childhood of author Jeannette Walls. I knew instantly this excerpt was going to become a reading lesson and a writing prompt. It would offer my student with the credit card, and all the others, something bigger to ponder in a season of gift-giving.

As I got ready to read this scene from Walls' sometimes shockingly bleak story, I reassured myself that it had been edited for seventh graders. It began with the author describing herself growing up poor and rootless in desert towns of the West, under the tutelage of her eccentric parents. Looking back to the Christmas when she was 5, Walls wrote, "I never believed in Santa Claus. None of us kids did. Mom and Dad refused to let us." Probably motivated by the fact that they didn't have enough money to fill Christmas stockings for their three children, Jeannette's parents waved away any notion that someone would slide down the chimney and deliver presents.

Instead of tangible gifts, Jeannette's father had another idea. On Christmas Eve, he took his children one by one into the backyard under the diamond-studded darkness of the night sky. He talked to them about quasars, and black holes and light years. He had already taught them to steer by the North Star, and they could identify some constellations.

Now, looking up at these familiar points of light, he told each child they could have any star they wanted. It was his gift. Scoffing at the notion of toys made by a band of elves at the North Pole—especially when they bore labels such as, "Made in Japan"—Jeannette's father told them that when those toys were broken and forgotten, "you'll still have your stars."

I loved this story and when I read it aloud in class it was obvious the kids did, too. "What was the nature of the father's gift?" I asked. In every class, kids found their way to the nugget of gold in the message: Mr. Walls had given his children his time, his knowledge, his warmth, his love, something from his heart.

I asked my students to try to remember presents they had given or received that could not have been purchased in a store. At first, nobody could think of anything.

Finally one remembered her grandmother making a scrapbook for her of old family pictures. Another recalled a little brother offering a gift-wrapped drawing. Soon the floodgates opened; examples ranged from handed-down watches and jewelry to toddler performances, handwritten poems, and much more. Our discussion focused on the heightened meaning of a gift that was more than a click online, a gift that carried within it the time and creative expression of the giver. I asked students to open their journals and write about getting just such a gift. I was feeling very proud to know that shortly I would send these kids off into the suffocating materialism of the holiday season with Jeannette Walls' story in their heads and in their hearts.

That was until the next day when the principal called me down to talk about an angry email he had gotten from the mother of one of my students.

"What have you done now?" Dave asked me in a teasing voice. "Telling these innocent 13-year-olds there is no Santa Claus?" Clearly he wasn't too upset even if the writer of the email obviously was.

He read from it: "I knew one day that my daughter would learn about Santa Claus. But it never occurred to me to think that one of her schoolteachers would be the one to steal her childhood."

We both knew the mother to be a malcontent, constantly berating and bullying teachers on a Facebook page. "This isn't going anywhere," Dave said, looking up from the computer screen, "but tell me what happened."

Thinking of that mother helped me recall the frown and grumbling her daughter displayed in class that day. That reaction was no surprise because she often sounded a sour note in response to class activities. It was her way of getting attention. It would never have occurred to me that she or any other seventh-grader maintained the Santa myth at home.

As I explained Walls' excerpt to Dave and laid out the lesson that I thought it showed, he watched my confidence and enthusiasm drain away. I was actually trembling when I left his office after we finished. But this incident wasn't over.

A day or so later, checking my mail cubby near the main office, I discovered a small package wrapped in brown paper with an unfamiliar return address in New York. Another present to open, I thought, as I tore the taped end of it. The box had a weight I couldn't immediately associate with a typical teacher gift: too heavy for a mug—maybe a paperweight?

Inside, lay a white box, taped closed, and a note written in aggressive, slanted script, its black marker message addressing me by name:

"Shame on you for not believing. Now you will receive what any naughty little girl gets in her stocking. Maybe in the future you will find the Christmas spirit."

Its falsely familiar tone and threatening, off-kilter message scared me. I opened the box cautiously. Packed inside were charcoal briquettes like dirty, black Easter eggs, leaving a dark smudge on the inside of the white top.

Thoroughly rattled, I went back to Dave's office and showed him the note and package. He was quiet at first. Then he called in the school security officer, held out the box of "coal" and described the mother's angry email. After examining the postmark and reading the email, the officer surprised us.

"I went to school with her—and her husband," he said. "Or ex. They're divorced." He looked again at the postmark: a town on Long Island. "That's where he lives."

I shuddered involuntarily and turned to Dave.

"Please," I said, "take their daughter out of my class."

"I know. You're upset," Dave said softly. "Think about it over the weekend."

As my anxiety worsened, I confided in my friend Libby, and she suggested I show the box to my postmaster on the way home. The post office clerk, busy with a long line of customers with holiday packages to mail, said he would refer it to the postal inspectors.

Ultimately, nothing was done about the anonymous box—or the student who seemed to gloat after that day, surely aware what her parents had done. I kept the charcoal and note in a cupboard in my room for weeks, thinking some new information might surface, but each time I saw the package I got the creeps again. Finally I threw it away.

I also threw away any thought of ever again using Jeannette Walls' story.

Happy holidays.

So, here I was this year, and the surge of pre-holiday excitement frothing around me needed to be harnessed. I was pretty confident about *A Christmas Carol* as an in-class live performance. And almost as soon as the books were passed around the kids' amped-up energy swung toward the play.

They began calling out.

"I want to be Scrooge."

"Please, let me be Scrooge."

"No, me, me, me."

My hand went up like a stop sign. "Whoa! Anyone who asks for a role will assuredly not get it!"

Groans.

"There are six acts, and at least one new Scrooge will be cast in each one. But there are other great parts for ghosts, and singers and lovesick ladies."

"I want that, I want that, the lovesick lady," shouted Cameron.

I glared at him.

"Oops. I forgot not to ask," he mumbled as his friends hooted.

"If some of you only know Scrooge as a Disney duck you are in for a treat," I said. "The only rule is: Come in on time and give your part the drama it deserves!"

Like a short-order cook, I began slinging roles right and left—the bell-ringer, the person who reads the stage directions and everything in-between. I also needed to assign a cappella singing to a student willing to be a little girl on the street with her doll. An attention-hungry boy with a sense of comedy would relish that role.

Kids were given little time to quibble. Once everyone had a part, I started the countdown: Five, four, three, two, (lights dimmed), one... you're on.

The prologue set us in Victorian England. It was snowing, and people were bustling about the streets as Ebenezer Scrooge grumbled in his shop. Silence bound the class as kids prepared, looking for their parts, fingers tracing their lines, lips forming the words silently to be sure they could pronounce them. One by one, they tried to outdo each other with fake British accents, spitting complaints, hurling insults, purring compliments.

In no time, they became captive to the wonder of the world they'd entered. Wonder fuels learning, of course. You don't have to be a teacher to recognize the awe in children as they look at the ordinary world.

Every little bug or pebble is a marvelous discovery.

As a columnist for an airline magazine when my son was young, I devoted one monthly piece to the discoveries he and a friend made on an unforgettable walk. I called them Lewis and Clark. Carrying a magnifying glass the boys marched ahead, stopping over and over to examine a crack in the sidewalk, a flattened can, a lady bug, until finally we arrived at a murky woodland stream. All at once, I noted in my column, "we noticed a narrow wake in the center of the water coming our way...A silky head rose gracefully..." The boys saw whiskers and wet fur. The head disappeared in a wink but time stopped as we absorbed the image, hypnotically repeating, "We saw an otter!"

It was something like this kind of wonder I wanted my kids to experience during our visit to Victorian London.

Each student had a part, even the challenged ones. I gave a silver bell to a stumbling reader, Lance, to wag each time the script called for the tinkling sound of street music. It was a great role for a kid who would otherwise be left out. After all, he had to follow the script to ring the bell at the proper times, and that counted as reading. Special education kids who struggle with reading and writing often get skipped over. Not here. Lance had a role—kind of an important one. The other kids looked to him at the right moments. He became Lance the Bellman.

I learned the critical importance of inclusion firsthand from an adult acquaintance, who laid bare the shame of struggling to compensate for the dyslexia that rendered him a non-reader when he was young. Talking about this at a dinner party one night as we sat side-by-side, he said that after high school a friend gave him a copy of *One Flew over the Cuckoo's Nest*. "And I sat down and read it." He couldn't explain exactly how he'd been able to but added, "I said to myself, 'I'm not dumb. Actually, I'm smart.'" He said that he is never without a book these days.

Back in the classroom, another non-reader waited by the row of open lockers. She would slam them on cue—bang, bang, bang—whenever the thunder clapped and the ghost of Marley appeared.

I knew the noise and spectacle of *A Christmas Carol* would be irresistible to seventh-graders, and quickly got past my initial twinge—that any production this complicated could quickly turn to disaster. What if students rejected it and staged a revolt or made fun and turned the reading into a parody? What if they couldn't pronounce the words? I needn't have worried.

The kids reading parts astounded me. Students who had often been silent, disengaged bolted forward showing an expressiveness I hadn't foreseen. Usually boisterous personalities settled into subtle, interpretative readings. A sarcastic boy in the back stretching out his long legs, suddenly sat up straight like a watchdog, waiting for his cue. The class pessimist, the fatalist, the showoff all had their roles. In sometimes soft, plaintive voices other times with Cockney slang they brought their lines to life.

Which brings me to Scrooge's most famous line. Without his asking, I could tell that a particularly gentle, rosy-cheeked kid, more like a velvet stuffed animal than an actual boy, wanted to play Scrooge's part. It seemed incongruous to imagine him as the sharp-tongued miser, but I gave it to him. Almost instantly, he took on a loud, insulting tone, banged the desk with his fist and shouted, "Christmas! Bah! Humbug!" None of us, including me, ever looked at him the same way again.

Another unexpectedly fortuitous bit of casting: A girl who never wanted the spotlight, Patricia, took on the role of the young Scrooge's sweetheart. Without blinking she was in it, heart and soul, tenderly asking, "Could you love me, Ebenezer?" We were all helplessly pulled in, readily believing that the familiar girl at the next desk was actually a heartsick young woman about to see her dreams dashed in a faraway time and place.

Totally absorbed, no one looked to the window now for snowflakes or watched the clock. In fact, if the bell rang before we got to a certain part, that kid would wail, "No fair. I was about to read!"

"We'll get to every scene," I promised, reminding them that we had a few days left to read.

The next day kids raced back to their desks, found the place in the script and prepared for showtime. Moved, as we were, by the strange beauty of each other's voices, they ignored it whenever someone tripped over a word or phrase and prompted each other in whispers: "Caleb... Caleb...that's you."

Our story was no cartoon version. In Dickens' powerful original, Marley in chains responds to Scrooge's question about what business the ghost has with him. "Much," he replies. Without prompting, and encountering this scene for the first time, our classroom Marley drew out the word—"Muuuuuuch"—and gave it a low, smoky, eerie sound. Our Scrooge caught his breath.

Finally, on Christmas morning when Scrooge orders the huge turkey sent to the Cratchits' house, the whole class spontaneously stood, ready to read together with Tiny Tim, "God bless us everyone."

"Are we allowed to say that?" Cameron asked

"It's okay," I answered. "It's in the story."

We had traveled across an ocean and back in time. We had met with ghosts, grieved for an abandoned boy and a love affair lost, cast a gimlet eye at the consequences of greed. Between acts students had actually displayed the same anxiety expressed by the original readers of Dickens' serialized tale, asking with furrowed brow whether Tiny Tim survives.

"He doesn't die, does he?" The question came from our bellringer, Lance.

Across the hall, students sat silently in a darkened room watching an animated movie. Here we were ready to sail off into the sparkly holidays on a wave of imagination.

When the buses pulled out, I began to think about heading home to get going on that aspic. As I was straightening up and pulling together paperwork for the next unit, Donnell passed my door with her scarf wrapped around her neck and her canvas bag heavy with student papers.

"See you next year," I called out. She grunted some kind of response that I couldn't make out. Probably a complaint about the weather. The snow was picking up, filling the Connecticut woods outside our big classroom window just as it had the London streets.

# EIGHT

# Into Deep Water

It was a new year and my classroom was ready. Before leaving for the holiday break I had set everything up for the unit that would greet the kids when they came back: the Titanic. A 4-foot long cardboard ship model we would use had been dusted off and was now docked on a rolling cart at the front of the room.

Clusters of rearranged desks represented First Class, Second Class, Third Class and ship's crew, including the captain, telegraph officer, lookout, and a ship musician. I had made copies of passenger lists and pictures of elegant staterooms as well as steerage compartments, and, importantly, Titanic boarding passes. The first thing students would see was a "Welcome Aboard" sign hung over the doorway and the homemade luxury liner, a prop that one student had brought in a few years earlier. Then each got a boarding pass.

More than almost anything else, seventh-grade kids enjoy this sort of personalized virtual experience. I had seen that with the Dickens reading and many other times. It was as if they became older and wiser when they took on adult acting roles.

A similar transformation occurred years earlier as we concluded a unit of reading biographies by staging a "dinner party." Across a table, posing as the famous people they read about, kids conversed and asked each other questions.

Our version of Andrew Carnegie wondered whether Eleanor Roosevelt ever felt confined in the role of first lady. Orville Wright and Abraham Lincoln batted around ideas about advances in transportation.

There were no costumes, the food was simple and the silverware plastic—and yet their conversation made the banquet seem more real than pretend. The tenor was sober and seemingly spontaneous. I remember Albert Einstein asking Harriet Tubman whether she had considered not taking the risk of going back to help other slaves after her own escape. "Certainly not!" Tubman answered instantly and with force. "The whole point of my life was to save as many people as I could. It was my cause."

Reenactments help students retain more than mere facts about their characters. They learn and remember how hard it was for Marie Curie to get an education, how determined Helen Keller was to make a speaking tour. Activities like this infuse life and meaning into lessons that otherwise could be as boring as canned soup.

I stopped by the ship to flatten a piece of tape back onto the deck. I was happy for our Titanic "voyage" to be nearly underway and pretty sure it would excite everyone, including a girl named Gabrielle who had shown up in my class a month earlier with no academic records and little background information.

Even my mentor Deborah—who no longer questioned the future success of Amir and had Chenlee starting to chat in English—paused with concern over Gabrielle. Deborah feared we might not be able to offer all the help this new student needed. Bone-thin Gabrielle stared at the floor or covered her face and always kept her distance. It was hard to tell how much she understood or knew. Her answer to everything was, "I don't know."

Finally, I needed to address this habit. I asked her privately, "Do you like sitting in the front of the class?"

"I don't know."

"Do you like reading?"

"I don't know."

Her words created a hiding place, I suspected, and soon learned that this metaphor had a literal parallel in her life: Gabrielle, her mother and little sister were living in a safe house, literally concealing themselves from her abusive father. Their whole world was a hiding place.

One day when I noticed Gabrielle still didn't have any supplies of her own, I asked, "Would you like this extra journal?"

"I don't know."

I decided to try a lighter approach, and even kid her a little.

"Gabrielle, we need to take care of something," I said, after most of the kids had left for lunch. "It's the 'I don't know' thing. We need to diversify." I had a serious look on my face, but then smiled. She listened as I continued.

"It's boring. It's not helpful. We need to have some other choices."

She eyed me curiously.

"Instead of 'I don't know' you could say, 'I'm not sure.'"

I cocked my head as she contemplated that choice. "That option buys some time without agreeing to anything. Or, you could say, 'I need to think about it.' Another good choice. Or, even, 'Maybe.' Or, 'What do you think?'"

She seemed vaguely interested, so I grabbed a legal pad and began to list the options, with a number by each.

"Here are some choices. We'll keep these on hand as a reminder. How about that?" As Gabrielle's finger gently slid down the page, she looked up at me.

"I don't know," she said.

"Oops," my voice went low with exaggerated concern. "That's not on the list. How about another choice?"

"I don't know," she said quickly.

"Uh-oh," I said looking at her with a broad smile. "Not on the list."

The tiniest shadow of a smile touched her lips. Her lowered eyes scanned the page up and down. I waited.

"I'm not sure," she said. The words came out so softly. But she had left the security of the shore and was moving toward open water. This is what we'd be doing as a class, but I couldn't help thinking that, in the wide ocean, ships sometimes go down. Before our Titanic sails, let me tell one more story about this fragile passenger, Gabrielle.

One day, some time later, she arrived early for homeroom, dropped her books, covered her face and burst out crying. No other students had come in yet. I quickly dodged desks to get to her, but she turned away, wiping her nose, her whole body shuddering.

"What happened? What happened?" I asked, my mind racing through the very worst possible scenarios. Was her mother okay?

Gabrielle wrapped her arms around her slim body, locking herself off.

"Please let me take you to the counselor's office," I whispered, as students began to arrive, fanning out around the room, noisily chatting.

She kept shaking her head. "No. No. No. No." Whatever it was she couldn't tell anybody. It would be a dam break.

"Okay," I said. "You must come for lunch so we can talk." I tried to make it sound like an order, but a friendly one. After the Pledge of Allegiance, the bell rang for the first class, and she disappeared down the hall. My fingers were crossed that Gabrielle would show up for lunch.

When she did appear, carrying her lunch tray, eyes averted, she took a seat and I settled into a desk nearby. I handed her a tissue.

"Tell me," I said softly. She stared at her tray for a moment.

Gabrielle began in a mournful whisper: "My sister came home yesterday. It was her birthday." She took a shallow breath. "She didn't know it was her birthday."

My mind screeched to a halt. Oh my god. Her sister, in third grade, did not know when her own birthday was. Her mother did not mention that special event in the morning as her daughter got up. There were no presents, no cards, no special pancakes.

Gabrielle continued: "At school, her teacher knew." She glanced at me with a questioning look, then reached for a french fry from her tray and nibbled on it. "Her teacher gave her a cupcake. She gave the whole class a cupcake."

Gabrielle looked at me squarely now, still puzzled. She couldn't register how this personal information—her sister's date of birth—could have been public. Again she stared at her plate.

"When my sister got home, she came into the kitchen where we were, my mom and me. She was crying." She tore off a tiny bite from the end of the pizza triangle and tucked it into her mouth.

"My sister said, 'I didn't know it was my birthday. The teacher told me. She had cupcakes.'" Gabrielle's eyes narrowed. "She didn't even know."

Next, her mother did something that astonished Gabrielle—she went out to the car, drove to a store and came back.

"She brought her a doll. My mom never gave me a present. She never gave me a doll."

Gabrielle inhaled a sudden shudder sob, and new tears came. I reached into the box of tissues in my lap and handed her another one, touching her hand.

"Easy. Easy. You need to catch your breath." When I thought she was settling down, she spoke again.

"I found that doll," she said slowly, tensing and staring at her hands. "I took it into the bathroom." Her eyes blazed in an expression of anger and shame. "I pulled its head off."

Silence for a long time. When she spoke again, her voice had an edge to it.

"She never gave me anything."

Looking at the top of her head, I said a quick prayer for guidance.

The grief of this bird-thin little girl created such a wide gulf.

"But Gabrielle, she loves you," I said. "Your mother loves you. She is protecting you. She has a lot on her mind. She is your mother."

She took a last nibble of her cold pizza, saying nothing. We both exhaled. Somehow lunch was over.

Later that afternoon, when Gabrielle came to English class, I had a plan. She needed to move forward. I had colored paper, stickers, stamps, markers and an idea. All the other kids were writing in their journals. It was not at all uncommon for me to spend extra time sitting with a particular student, such as Gabrielle. Some students' assignments were modified, and the other kids got that.

"Let's have some fun," I whispered.

She turned to me, her dark eyes full of questions.

"Let's make a birthday card," I said. I knew how hard it was for almost any girl her age to resist sparkly stickers and colorful markers.

"What's your little sister's name?" When she hesitated, I added, "She'll love it."

Then, something came over the big sister who had beheaded the doll. She reached for a piece of pink paper and began to center a red heart sticker in the middle of it. And on she went. Whew.

Anyway, back to the classroom with the docked ship: We had navigated our way to the launch of the Titanic, and now we were moving out into deep water. The Titanic's story represented the perfect intersection of student interest and fact-loaded learning. In addition to the measurable particulars that made this tale so enticing—water temperature, ocean depth, longitude and latitude, financial value, miles, yards, feet, inches, hours, minutes—there was the breathtaking power of knowing the outcome of an epic tragedy while watching it unfold.

We read newspaper articles, journal entries, even part of the transcript of an inquest into the causes of the sinking. We also read from a book by Robert Ballard, the person who found the wreck seven decades after the ship sank to the bottom of the Atlantic. Ballard's book was *Discovering the Titanic*.

What I didn't know was that my own experience of this unit might have been called, *Discovering Caleb*.

There he sat, a puzzling, good-natured kid who often seemed to be deep in thought, gazing out our big window during class, his mind somewhere out there amid the trees. When I called on Caleb he was polite, but as baffled as someone coming out of a deep sleep. He would stare at me, eyes searching for any clue to the topic we were discussing. Nothing came.

His mother said he was discouraged by the poor grades he was getting. His father said he was very visual, "in fact, insanely good at drawing." He loved social studies, I was told. Try as I might, I could not keep his attention in my class.

Struggling learners were not new to me, of course. Often they'd already been diagnosed with learning disabilities and they came to us with a special plan to compensate. In addition to meeting with their parents and special education teachers, classroom teachers often received materials prepared by experts on a variety of disabilities ranging from hearing impairments to processing disorders as part of a constant effort to keep us up-to-date on practices and methods.

We learned to adapt for students diagnosed with autism, defiance disorder, depression, anxiety, various other emotional conditions, and more and more often ADD (Attention Deficit Disorder) and ADHD (which includes hyperactivity in addition to distractibility). It was an extraordinary challenge on top of our goal to deliver education to a given class of 25 kids, five times each day.

Caleb was not on a special-education plan, but the need for one was becoming obvious. His mind flitted away from the subject at hand after a minute of focusing. I put him in the front of the room. I paired him with the most attentive and helpful kid in class. I stayed nearby, tapped his desk when he drifted, put sticky notes of encouragement on top of his pile of books. I let him draw while I talked. But somehow I still couldn't get onto his mental agenda. The other teachers, too, were stymied by this boy.

Henry Curry, a spunky, retired fifth-grade teacher who often substituted for colleagues up and down the hall, knew Caleb well. At team meetings, Henry would lightly move on when someone mentioned Caleb's vacant stare, with a phrase: "He lives so far out, there's no ZIP code."

That changed as soon as I introduced our new unit. At the word "Titanic," oddly, amazingly, Caleb woke up. His eyes flashed open and his hand shot up.

"Can I wear a costume?" he asked.

"Yes!" I was emphatic. I had no idea what his costume might entail, and didn't care.

That first day, when I handed each kid a boarding pass copied from the original I found online, most of them immediately began buzzing. "What's this for?" "What are we doing?"

Caleb just studied his intently.

Kids found their seats and each opened an envelope containing the identity of a real passenger from the Titanic manifest. Some were children, even a baby; some were famous, like the fabulously rich John Jacob Astor IV, and Isidor Straus, the co-owner of Macy's.

The first task for my students was to write their new names on their boarding passes. They would not be allowed to enter class the next day without those tickets. One by one, students introduced themselves to the class and told their ages and whether they were First-, Second-, or Third-class passengers or part of the ship's crew. I made Gabrielle a safe, Second-class traveler and sat her among a small group of nice kids.

When I asked them about their prior knowledge of the Titanic's voyage, some remembered only the Leonardo DiCaprio-Kate Winslet movie.

"I loved Rose. Can I be Rose?" girls asked.

My response: "That was fiction. Rose was made up."

Some knew a handful of facts gathered from television specials and books. Others knew almost nothing.

Then there was Caleb. He swept into class wearing a bowler hat, a bow tie, a long black coat and a wide grin. Not once in the next two weeks would his attention stray. It turned out he knew everything there was to know about the great ship and brought in books, pictures, maps and artifacts to share with the class. At one point, he even drew a diagram of the Titanic on the whiteboard in intricate detail. He was a natural artist, as his father had said.

During our first exercise, "Titanic Jeopardy"—a takeoff on the long-running quiz show—Caleb tried hard to refrain from blurting out the right response before anyone else had a chance. I put eight numbers on the board and asked students to guess what they represented.

"I'll take 65," said one student. She guessed it was the number of babies aboard.

No.

Another guessed it was the number of crew members.

No.

Finally Caleb couldn't wait any longer. "It's the number of lifeboats."

Yes!

"What? Only 65 lifeboats?" someone cried out. Caleb looked around, nodding.

Who's next?

A hand went up. "I'll take the number 28. That's the day of the month it sank?"

No.

Finally, someone correctly guessed that 28 referred to the temperature of the iceberg-filled ocean water. An outraged chorus went up. "Wait. That's below freezing!" I explained that the ocean's salt kept it from freezing.

With each right answer, my students were unearthing the bones of this story; they were on a treasure hunt, and stumbling along the way became part of the sport.

Right in there with the others, sometimes offering the answer but not hogging the show, was Caleb, in his bowler. Later, during a team meeting, Ben, the math teacher, asked, "What the heck is Caleb doing walking around in a hat and raincoat?"

"It's our Titanic unit. He's in character. Please let him wear it," I said. "He's on fire for the subject." Ben and everyone else agreed to go along. We teachers trusted each other.

Back in my class, Caleb was Mr. Astor, possibly the richest man in the world. (I had rigged the cards to give him that role, which I knew would delight him). He surveyed the desks surrounding him as if scanning the deck chairs of the ship. He knew his way around. The very same rich imagination that had drawn him away from the classroom before now drew him back in. He was fully employed.

After the Ballard excerpt, we read distress telegraph messages—among the earliest S.O.S. calls ever—and I handed out an article from an English newspaper. It revealed that a lookout in the crow's nest finally spotted the iceberg with just his eyes: An earlier lookout had absent-mindedly pocketed the key to the telescope cabinet. Shocked awareness swept across my classroom. No key. No telescope.

Kids looked at each other as I passed around an old metal skeleton key that I'd brought from home. They wrapped their fingers around it and inhaled audibly. "Is this the key?" one asked. I told him it was similar.

At the inquest the lookout was asked, "If you had the telescope could you have seen the iceberg sooner?"

"Yes," he replied.

"In time?"

"I think so."

Eyes widened around the room. This was getting real.

We read the poem, "Convergence of the Twain" by Thomas Hardy, about the iceberg's fateful formation even as the ocean liner took shape at a shipyard.

> *And as the smart ship grew*
> *In stature, grace, and hue*
> *In shadowy silent distance grew the iceberg, too.*

The 1912 poem, written to help raise money for families of those lost, included words unfamiliar to today's seventh graders. One line asks, "What does this vaingloriousness down here?" When I asked the class what the poem was about, some weren't sure. Caleb, of course, was happy to explain.

When we finally, reluctantly reached the end of the Titanic unit, it was time for each passenger to learn his or her individual fate. I read the roll call and solemnly informed them one by one.

"Millvina Dean."

"Yes?"

"You survived."

Millvina exhaled, "Oh. Whew."

"Mr. Straus."

"Yes?"

"I'm sorry, you didn't make it."

Students patted Mr. Straus on the shoulder.

Caleb's alter ego also perished. He knew that, of course, and took it well. After all, he had gallantly gone down with the ship, while his young bride had gotten a place on a lifeboat and survived.

It was over. I would put away the ship model. We'd be on to something else, setting sail as just a regular class again. I couldn't help wondering: Had Caleb possibly come aboard for good?

# NINE

# What is Freedom?

Beyond our classroom windows, the silhouettes of dark trees looked as if they had been punched out of the stark white sky. The once-welcoming woods had closed itself off. And it wasn't just the late winter landscape that was bleak. It was also the news that came, in sad whispers.

We had just learned, through the teacher grapevine, that Lindsey's 19-year-old sister had died of a drug overdose in Florida. That instantly awakened a memory: A friend of mine had lost her son the same way years ago, and I recalled the agony her family had faced before the end. Surely all fall, I imagined, Lindsey's family had endured the same torture, watching their oldest child slip away as drugs took over and she withdrew, declining to let them help, refusing to answer their phone calls—just as my friend's son had. Perhaps her mother or father had traveled to Florida, made arrangements for detox, tried to intervene. No doubt, the younger sisters huddled together to listen to desperate late-night conversations between their parents. Now, crushing grief displaced that crushing fear.

Foolishly, I had always assumed that elite soccer players like Lindsey and her sisters were somehow immune to drug addiction. With a large dose of what looked like confidence, Lindsey had dismissed our class novel with a flip of her ponytail in the first month of school, triggering my lecture about sports and school and me being the English "coach."

Libby, Deborah, Donnell, and I arrived at the church together and found a place near the back, with Donnell at the end of the pew. Always in charge, she had insisted on driving, of course. Up front, Lindsey and her sisters looked so small and blank-faced, just arm's length from their big sister's coffin.

After the service we waited outside to hug the girls. "Those poor kids," someone said on our mostly silent drive home. Every year brought pivotal moments that reminded me how staggeringly difficult life can be for us all, young and old. But this year had more grief in store.

Cancer, we learned, had returned and taken our beloved Henry Curry, that gem of a Catholic-school-educated, tie-wearing teacher with his jaunty style and rich sense of humor. Years before, on my first day at the school, Henry had slowed down in the hall to salute me by name with a crisp, "Good morning," and then: "Welcome to another day in paradise." All the teachers looked forward to that daily greeting.

Henry returned as a substitute after he retired and peppered our seventh- grade teacher meetings with wisecracks. We'd share updates on students: Mac's been to the nurse three times today for no apparent reason, Cameron's mother is complaining about his grades, Jimmy Grady cheated on his math quiz.

"We all know Jimmy is headed for the state pen. We can't fix that one," Henry would say with an impish twinkle in his eye. As to Cameron's science grade, "That was a very generous C," he said, lowering his eyebrows and voice for emphasis. "Very generous."

A few minutes later when someone tried to bring up Jimmy Grady again, Henry put up a stop sign hand. "Jimmy's still in the parking lot." This bit of often-ridiculed jargon, picked up at a professional workshop, was meant to sideline irrelevant topics.

"Long-term parking," intoned Ben, the math teacher who rarely joined in the merriment. Libby let out a hoot.

Now Henry was gone. After his death, emails full of memories and stories started coming in from some of the thousands of kids who had passed through his classes. One remembered him standing on his desk to deliver a lesson, another loved "the crazy music he played"—the crooning torch songs from the 1940s that I looked forward to hearing when I passed his room. One note described "feeling important when Mr. Curry called me sir or addressed me as mister."

As a soothing gesture for us teachers, one friend ordered plastic bracelets inscribed, *Another Day in Paradise*. We would twirl them around and around during meetings, subconsciously, I guess, when we got mired in a bog of double-speak.

That winter's bad news wasn't finished. A few weeks later, our counselor, Mr. D, delivered a somber report to all the teachers on my team. A student, Carla, would be out for a couple of weeks; her mother had found her computer searches with the key word "suicide."

*She what? How could this be possible?* I remembered Carla rushing into our homeroom after the holidays thrilled to breathlessly tell that she'd managed—by jumping up and down—to get on the New Year's Eve Times Square telecast. Now she was in a private psychiatric hospital. We teachers would put her homework assignments in a folder in the office.

Again it struck me how fragile some seventh graders are in this pivotal year. As I've said, "unguarded" is another way to put it. More perceptive than sixth graders and less jaded than eighth graders, they still floated in a tilting bubble of hope. To be simultaneously hopeful and aware is to inhabit a precarious perch. I steadied myself by recalling the others—the kids who arrived in seventh grade with a sturdy sense of self and a maturity the others hadn't reached yet.

To entice both groups I often began a new reading assignment with a pointed, often startling question to the class. When we prepared to read a thrilling non-fiction account of an infant who crawled onto a railroad track as a freight train bore down, only to be nudged safely aside by the conductor's foot, I asked, "Is it ever a good idea to kick a baby?"

Similarly, my set-up for the Langston Hughes' tale "Thank You M'am" was, "Have you ever wanted something bad enough to break the law to get it?" And for Shirley Jackson's short story "Louisa, Please Come Home" (about a girl who ran away from home and changed her identity), I asked, "Has anyone ever considered running away?"

Most of the faces in front of me looked dismayed if not offended by that question. Run away? Never! their eyes instantly told me. A disappointed murmur accompanied their disapproving glances—until one voice broke in.

"Oh, yes. All the time." It was Kate. Around her there were gasps and raised eyebrows, but she was unmoved.

"I could fend for myself. I could live under a bridge if I had to." More whispers and shaking of heads. Kate, who had an overly cautious twin brother, imagined herself in a life of daring and risk. She couldn't wait to get there.

Lara, another student, detached herself from the class in a different but equally imaginative way. In a perceptive and original piece of writing, she described herself as a "spy in seventh grade," unnoticed but always watching and learning from the action around her.

Reading that, it instantly dawned on me that I, too, felt like a spy. I was witnessing the unfolding of a great story: seventh grade. Ear to the wall. I couldn't help reviewing the events of each day in my own mind and recording them at night in my journal, like a dossier. It was clandestine intelligence-gathering. But this story was not just about kids and comments and what we heard. It was about the extraordinary exchange taking place.

In my mind, I went back to things I'd learned in teacher training, back to John Dewey, who emphasizes that school is not an information dump. Shoveling content—"bits of geography," Dewey sniffed—mattered less to him than encouraging inquiry, modeling a love of learning, and inspiring creative thinking. To describe what takes place between a teacher and a student Dewey had used that word "transaction."

Teachers who exaggerated the importance of content baffled me. Was the idea that this was like armor or equipment to use when students got out into the real world? Weren't they already in the real world? A world in which kids were confined to psychiatric wards, and sisters died, and mothers went to jail? "Education is not preparation for life," Dewey said, "education is life itself." Hell, yes.

What would this philosopher think of the test-taking treadmills that many of today's schools have become? Mightn't a sense of being trapped or off-balance contribute to the all-too-common drug overdoses, the thoughts about suicide? Thirteen-year-olds could so easily feel hemmed in by society, ensnared by the barbed requirements of conformity.

Lucky me. My class offers, I thought, a formula for our way out. Literature provides a virtual escape from every confining experience and presents solutions for real-life problems without real-life risk. What better road to wisdom than the perfect story or poem? It delivers without strings. It isn't bossy. There's no "told you so." Instead there is a sense that one has arrived at an understanding on one's own. Ownership. Buy-in. How important are all these things?

But literature is a magic carpet ride only if the reader lets it sweep him or her away.

With that thought in mind, the image of a boy named Alexander popped into my head. This top-notch math and science scholar was simply disengaged in my class. His mother was desperate to learn why he didn't earn an A in English. Simple: There was no buy-in. He read for content only, for information, seeking facts and never letting his feelings get involved. Alexander's writing was brief, unoriginal, flat and yet, he presented a superior attitude. How could I pierce the Teflon exterior that restrained him?

Then one day I looked up to see this usually inexpressive young man really laughing. One of his friends had made a comment that amused him, no doubt, but his blurting laugh was incongruous.

"What's happened?' I asked in a teasing tone. "Alexander, what's come over you?"

He shrugged and, giggling again, put his head on the desk, his narrow shoulders bobbing up and down. He really couldn't stop the bubbling bursts.

Seizing the moment, I renamed him.

"Okay, Mr. Bubbles, let's get a grip. Settle down."

He picked his head up, his face shining with merriment and let out another burst of laughter. He was helpless, and thereafter he had a new name.

A light-hearted Mr. Bubbles took the place of the stoical Alexander. I can't say that he became a passionate reader or a great writer, but his rigid approach to English class vanished. Magically, I had access to Mr. Bubbles in a way I never had to Alexander.

Thinking back to my own junior high school, I know I could never have laughed like that in class. How liberating is it for kids this age to feel that free? Does freedom invite courage—the courage to discard toxic acquaintances and make new friends, to try a new sport, take on a hobby that isn't cool, show you care about something or someone who isn't popular? Does freedom help shape a kid's individuality, allowing him or her to reason independently, think originally and at a new depth—not like a child anymore?

It was time to bring out two wonderfully rich poems that would allow the class to explore the concept of freedom: one about an elephant, by Rudyard Kipling, the other about a turtle, by Mary Oliver.

The Kipling poem seems almost childish at first, describing a tethered, working elephant in India who longs for the old days when he was free and who revisits his lost loves in dreams at night.

*I will remember what I was.*
*I am sick of rope and chain—*
*I will remember my old strength*
*and all my forest affairs.*

Oliver's poem, "The Turtle," describes the fierce, instinctive journey of a sea turtle as she goes ashore to lay her eggs. She is so connected to the sand and to the birds above that there is almost a string between them.

*She can't see*
*herself apart from the rest of the world*
*or the world from what she must do*
*every spring.*

For this lesson I would start with a simple question, one that would feel unchallengingly comfortable—until, I hoped, some perceptive 13-year-old would peel back the edges and see that there was more there. I counted on this imagined pioneer to lead the class in a voyage of discovery.

So after reading both poems aloud, with the kids tracking the lines on their copies, I paused and asked, "Which of these animals is free?"

Only a moment passed before a hand went up.

"Well, the elephant has 'rope and chain,'" said Cameron, who was beginning to drive me a little less crazy. "So he clearly isn't free." He looked down at the second poem.

"It has to be the turtle. Obviously, the turtle," he said smiling, happy he'd made an easy catch in the first seconds of the ballgame.

Others murmured, "Yes, the turtle."

"How do you know that?" I challenged.

Cameron continued to run with the ball.

"Well, she has no chains. She can swim to the sand and lay her eggs and look around," he answered.

I scanned the classroom with an expression suggesting there might be more going on here. Students are self-trained to watch the teacher for such clues. Another hand.

"It can't be the elephant because look at the way man controls the elephant," said Hailey. "He is a slave for man. On the other hand, the turtle is living in nature, completely following her own path."

Heads nodded. We were moving toward consensus.

In a quick glance out our big window, I saw a bird pass by over the woods. I wanted this discussion to take flight. A conversation like this could die if kids believed I would let it die.

"Is physical freedom the only kind of freedom?" I asked.

Slowly, Richard raised his hand. He had come a long way since he willingly let sixth graders ravage his essay for mistakes a few months earlier.

"There is something to be said for the freedom the elephant has to dream or think at night about his life and past." He spoke tentatively at first.

I'd never listened more closely. He went on.

"It's true, he doesn't have physical freedom, but he may have an even more important kind of freedom—the freedom to think and remember and dream."

An almost imperceptible intake of breath swept across the room.

Cameron piped up. "Maybe they are both free, in a sense." He believed he was staying in the game.

I looked back at Richard to see if he would take this up.

"Maybe not," Richard said. "Look at these words used to describe the turtle: *to complete what she was born to do.*"

He looked around. "Sounds like destiny. Like she has no choice."

"And look at this," he continued, reading: "*She's only filled with an old blind wish. It isn't even hers…"*

Tracing his finger down the lines of the poem, he read: *"she doesn't dream…"*

The class was silent.

Richard looked up. "How is a creature considered free if it can't dream or 'doesn't' dream?"

I turned to the class.

"What does the ability to dream represent?" I asked.

Juliana's hand went up for the first time in this kind of exploratory discussion. She was my "sergeant-at-arms" in homeroom, tidying up the student supply area, helping with attendance, erasing the board each day. But she stayed on the sidelines in intellectual free-for-alls like this.

"I'm not sure what it means," she started. "But, it might represent a state of consciousness beyond the day-to-day reality. If the turtle doesn't dream…" Juliana trailed off.

"Yes?" I encouraged.

"Well, if she doesn't dream, she is tied to the present. She can't choose. There are no other options."

Juliana glanced at the others. "Maybe the turtle is captive in both ways," she continued. "In her body and in her mind. Controlled by instinct."

I felt a flutter of joy. Caterpillar to butterfly. Juliana was unfurling her wings, pushing out of the chrysalis. She was stirring awake.

Cameron said, "So maybe she isn't even physically free if she's just…like, programmed by destiny."

One of his buddies rapped his shoulder from behind. "Destiny?" he asked. "That's Richard's word. You don't even know that word!"

Cameron shrugged.

Way in the back of the class I caught the rare sight of a shifting movement at Logan's desk. He generally kept his thoughts to himself.

His hand went half-way up and retracted.

"Yes, Logan?" I said.

He shook his head. I needed to make sure kids felt safe enough to push the edges of this conversation. I bought time by talking.

"We are now examining what constitutes freedom," I summed up as I began to stroll outside the U of desks. "You have talked about different versions of freedom. Some of you have picked up on certain words or concepts like 'dreaming' that guide you. That's always a great way to get a purchase on an idea or a message." I circled back to the front of the room.

"Or, sometimes you bounce those ideas off your own experience to see what that reveals."

Logan raised his hand again. This time he spoke.

"Well, this may be way off-base." His voice was tentative.

"Maybe completely off-topic. But remember in social studies when Ms. Gibbens told us about the slaves from Africa who lost their freedom and she said that we, kids like us, take it all for granted. We don't even realize we're free."

He looked around to gauge the reactions. "This just reminded me of that. We don't even have the awareness of freedom. Maybe we are somewhere between the elephant and the turtle."

"Hmm," Bronwyn mused almost to herself. "Is it still freedom if you don't even know you have it?"

Over near the bank of windows, where the sun had broken through the white sky, Lindsey summoned the courage to speak about something I could tell had been coming together in her mind as our discussion built.

"Or, maybe," she ventured, "some of us actually are slaves—kind of like the turtle—but we don't know it. We follow the demands of society to wear certain brand names like Nike, Abercrombie, Gap." She blushed, but continued.

"We want to belong, so we follow without questioning. We can't find our own path." She was in a free-fall of trust, like that game where you know the other person will catch you.

"Yeah, yeah," Jack O'Hara blurted. "I was just thinking how my dad always wanted me to play football. Always. 'Cause he loved football and watched it all the time. I went along until…" He stopped.

"It was like I wasn't free to choose my own sport. Until one day I just told him, I said, 'Maybe this isn't my sport, Dad.'"

"What did he say?" Cameron asked in an unusually quiet voice.

"He didn't really answer, but he took me off the roster for the team. He was the coach." There was a murmur as kids exchanged glances.

"The good thing is now I play baseball, the sport I love. That's freedom, and it's very important to me."

I remembered back in September when Jack said he wanted to write about baseball. Now I understood that choice was actually his declaration of independence.

Every single student was listening closely—maybe some were standing at similar crossroads. Surely, some were closer to the reckoning moment than others, but all of them felt the sometimes too-heavy guiding hand of a parent or teacher or just society—pushing them in a direction they hadn't chosen.

Across the room my eye fell on Hannah, nodding at Jack's words. Earlier in the week she had told me she didn't really like math, although she was good at it. "My parents want me to take advanced courses and major in math in college." Given her parents' situation, with all of the loose ends, their separate homes and psychologically wounded children, this divorced couple could at least agree on that. But she had earlier confessed to me privately, "What I really like is literature."

Richard drew my attention with a slight wave of his hand. "Back to dreaming," he said, elbows on the desk and hands folded.

"Human slaves dreamed. Like the elephant, they remembered who they used to be. They had independent consciousness, even when they were chained."

He was leading us deeper.

Bronwyn's turn: "In other words, knowing who you are is freedom, even if you can't act on it? Maybe. But I'd say it is only half of freedom. The other half is action."

Cameron was peering around the room with a dazed look on his face. This was the kid I used to pray would be absent; now I felt a tug of tenderness. I found myself smiling almost lovingly at him.

He finally spoke, mystified: "I thought these poems were about two animals. What just happened?"

# TEN

# A Purple Heart

Each year a new flock of students appears, and the whole job changes. It may sound crazy to say, but the kids, as a group, are quicker and brighter some years; other years they drag along, struggling to get the point. Happy years bring a slew of agreeable kids. Teeth-grinding years offer up more than the expected number of argumentative, contentious ones, often guided off-track by ringleaders like Cameron and his lieutenants.

Sometimes conflict erupts between students—girls as well as boys—who have long-standing feuds and need to be physically distanced from each other if they land in the same class. An unexpected challenge I had one year appeared in the form of a beautiful bully named Becca who silenced class discussions with a single eye roll.

All this had a powerful influence on the way a given year played out. Often I would be tipped off ahead of time by teachers of lower grades. Anna alerted me on Day One every year, keeping me posted on particular kids who had terrorized her sixth-grade classes.

On the other hand, the teaching staff was reliably stable in composition. Of course, there was always some social shifting; teachers are just like any other group of people. They don't always get along even though they try to act as if they do. Just like the kids in their classrooms, teachers gossip about each other, form cliques, strive for popularity and endure bullies in their own ranks.

In many schools there is a palpable rift between the veterans and the newest hires, the digital natives. This is a divide often aggravated by the relentless push from administrators for increased reliance on technology and data analysis. Uploading teacher self-evaluations, for example, had become akin to filing taxes, requiring grueling (for some of us) hours of marshaling endless digital "evidence."

On this stage of student melodrama, teacher friction and data-driven angst, arose a tragic scenario. One teacher's actions triggered the alarm of her peers. I guess you could say Donnell had stayed too long, like a veteran athlete who had begun to fumble. It was becoming clear to those closest to her that she was showing signs of burning out.

This showed up in many ways. For instance, at a seventh-grade team meeting I suggested we stop treating Seth like a bad little boy and start trying to find a way to engage him.

"We're gonna lose this kid," I said.

"No!" Donnell almost shouted. "I'll tell you what we can do with that little shit: Get rid of him. Send him to the office. Let those slackers deal with him." She shook her head and scowled.

The others exchanged quick, furtive looks that acknowledged how flammable this was. Yes, teachers are human beings and, yes, we sometimes use inappropriate language, but Donnell's tone went further. We all held our breath.

But on this occasion, someone in the group (I know who and I kind of understand) reported Donnell's language and demeanor to the principal. If there already was a file on her, it got thicker. It was as if we were watching the trail of an airplane with its engine on fire.

One day while walking by her classroom I heard her blasting voice directed at the boy we called Patrick Henry for his penchant for debate, who was sitting in the front row. He had refused to back down on some point and she wasn't going to let him win.

"Who do you think you are, trying to disrupt my class?" she roared. "When I tell you to stop talking, you shut up! Hear me?!" She was leaning dangerously close to Patrick. Her face was purple.

I did an instant U-turn and walked into her room. Donnell caught herself, almost mid-sentence, and began to control her breathing as we walked together to her desk. "What are you doing for lunch?" I asked off-handedly, as she slowly regained her composure. Teachers do this kind of intervention for each other when the situation warrants.

Teaching is a trying, stressful, exhausting job. Middle-school kids test our patience and stamina on a daily basis. When uncooperative kids push us to the brink, we need to decide whether to hold the line and insist on the rules (like making a student take down his hood) or whether to step back. We have to decide these things moment-to-moment—something Donnell had done for years. With a good night's sleep, a sense of humor and an effective seating chart, most of us manage to navigate the minefield.

That is, under regular circumstances. Then you have the tricky challenge of dealing with relentless kids like Patrick Henry, or defeated ones like Patricia, who had surrendered to a sense of failure. These were ordinary kids who at times became extraordinarily draining. Add in the children with formalized special-education plans—portfolios that require teachers to adapt the curriculum to their disabilities—and the stress level intensifies.

It depends on the kid, the moment, and the teacher. My colleague, Ben, at times had trouble making the right call. He was a wonderful math teacher, a character with corny jokes and glasses set low on his nose. He was authentic and original. Kids knew Ben was real. He loved his subject and he cared about his students, even though they might hurl wads of gum or pencils at the ceiling when he wasn't looking.

But Ben also could be too literal-minded about the protocols. Every year, experts called in by our special-education staff would brief teachers on the specific needs of incoming special-ed students and the particular accommodations required for each. I relished this meeting because Ben often showed these outside specialists what a classroom might look like if we followed their well-intentioned but sometimes clueless directives.

In meetings held before students return to school, classroom teachers face a rotating array of psychologists, counselors, special-ed personnel, teachers of the deaf, and nurses with information about extreme allergies, epinephrine injection pens (EpiPens) and seizures. The ESL folks (English as a Second Language) didn't present a program to actually teach English to non-English-speakers but offered advice for integrating those kids into regular classes—mostly by turning them over to Google. Ben listened closely to all this, trying to imagine following the directives. One briefing involved an incoming student afflicted with narcolepsy. We were told the boy might put his head down at any time and drift into a deep sleep.

"Do NOT disturb him," we were warned. He had what they termed a "pronounced startle reflex" and might have a seizure. But, also watch him closely, they added, because he could fall off his chair.

Ben, in his usual exacting style, responded.

"Just so I understand you. Jonathan will go to sleep in my class and I am not to wake him? Correct?"

"Correct," the specialist said.

"Okay, so how am I supposed to know exactly what he heard and didn't hear and how can I possibly keep him up with the class? What about the skills I'm teaching as he goes to sleep?"

The specialist advised checking in with the student the next day, positing that a gap in knowledge would show up on his homework sometime down the line.

Such bromides always set Ben off. He has a regular mantra about the nature of math—the stacking of skills, the learning progression, how each lesson built on a previous lesson. His kids needed to meet grade-level expectations on the standardized math tests, and if they didn't their failures reflected negatively on his own teaching record.

"I can't wait until I give a test to learn what Jonathan slept through," Ben said, his tone somewhere between sarcasm and desperation. "How can he tell me on Wednesday what he didn't hear on Tuesday? This is not going to work."

Silence. Crickets.

I loved it whenever Ben injected such slices of reality into these meetings. He just wanted to show the group what it looked like from a teacher's perspective. At the same time, I felt some sympathy for the experts because there was a plan they had to follow—the legally-mandated 504 (medical/physical) plan or the Individual Education Plan (IEP) handed to them by the previous year's special-ed teacher.

And we teachers were all sensitive to the obvious challenges that special-ed students faced. Always, there would be more meetings, and maybe some new ideas, perhaps novel drugs. More maturity in the student could sometimes miraculously change everything.

Two related groups of students merit mention here: The first includes kids who desperately need some accommodation but aren't "identified" for various reasons, often including reluctant parents. The other side of the coin involves perfectly capable kids whose parents maneuver to get them "labeled" and advantaged by a lighter academic load. These faux special-ed students are rare, thankfully.

In any event, requirements reign. Still, I rarely grappled head-on with the most unrealistic ones. I figured I'd get to know the student, and we would informally work things out. Talks with parents often helped. And our lessons themselves could help. Ours was an English class, after all, and our lessons relied on more subjective, intuitive, sometimes circular paths to understanding unlike math's ladder-like lessons requiring mastery of one specialized skill before moving on to the next.

Whenever a student showed no improvement over time, the teacher might try any number of new approaches. A paper trail was essential. We needed to keep records to measure the success or failure of a chosen strategy. These would be collated at the end of a given period and decisions would be made about specific adjustments.

My mind went back to one meeting in which we were told we needed to keep records for three weeks on a boy named Buddy whose "label" included attention-related issues. Like clockwork, Ben spoke up.

"Three weeks?"

Long pause.

"Do you have any idea how I am supposed to run a math class with 25 students while I am keeping these meticulous notes on Buddy's behavior moment-to-moment? How do you suggest I do this? Stop everything and walk over to my desk to find the chart and let the other kids enjoy a free-for-all, spitballs flying, while I take time to record Buddy's failure to attend? Really?"

Longer pause.

It turned out Buddy's was a delicate case. Teachers had come under fire for what his parents considered mishandling of their son. They demanded more sensitive management, insisting at the same time that he not be made to feel or look different—in spite of the fact that the school psychologist came into class regularly to monitor his behavior as well as the reactions of his teacher and other students.

Nobody liked what seemed to be busy work, but I immediately liked Buddy. At first, I even kind of enjoyed some of the stuff he blurted out in class. His impromptu comments were often random. (And, well, hadn't a friend once kidded me, saying, "You're the most random person I ever met"?) For a while, I also appreciated the provocative questions Buddy asked. But soon enough it became obvious that he had no awareness of the other students. Buddy thought he and I were the only two people in the room.

And yet, this boy was a learning machine. When he wasn't in school he was watching educational television specials, visiting museums or historic sites, or reading for hours. What Buddy lacked was people skills: experience in taking turns, sharing, listening, compromising. Students usually develop these skills in elementary school. How could a middle-school teacher bridge that gap? Whatever methods we tried, we were constantly under surveillance.

Meetings with Buddy's parents were harrowing. All his teachers had to attend, and it felt like Russian roulette. Who would get the bullet and for what alleged oversight?

Had any one of us made a seating chart change that inadvertently removed Buddy from the front row? Had we dealt too abruptly with him when he wouldn't stop disrupting class? I received an email one day from his mother complaining that he was being bullied by the boy at the next desk.

Good God! I had puzzled over that seating chart for hours because Buddy's class was loaded with problematic personalities. I had to keep the bully away from the professional victim, and the slob away from the kid with obsessive-compulsive disorder, the A student away from the cheater. I always worked in pencil and then erased, erased, erased. It was a human chemistry experiment: Put the wrong elements together and... POW!

Not many kids wanted to sit next to Buddy because he never stopped talking and often spilled over into their space with this arms and books and Ziploc snack bag. That said, Buddy was essentially a nice kid. Quite the contrary for finger-popping Mac, Mr. Negative. My seating arrangement had to start with Mac. His rudeness came in the form of constant insults, griping and grumbling under his breath—with comments like, "Who cares?" and "Duh." He irritated everyone.

I had learned that Mac had to be seated in the front of the class so I could keep a closer eye on him, but preferably at the end of the row with only one neighbor to annoy. After rejecting every other potential candidate, I put him next to Buddy, whose obliviousness to other kids, I figured, would protect him. What I hadn't calculated was that Mac would pepper Buddy with actual projectiles—tiny bits of crayon. Hence his mom's email. Back to the seating chart with my eraser.

At one meeting with Buddy's parents I was singled out again, but this time for praise. Apparently I had made Buddy feel good among his schoolmates.

I racked my brain for what I might have said, and the only thing I could remember was an exchange during a class discussion in which students described their reading habits. In typical fashion, Buddy expressed shock that anyone would have trouble reading a hundred pages in one sitting.

"I can finish a whole book in one day," he informed us.

All the kids we refer to as "reluctant readers" winced at the implied insult. I took a breath and faced Buddy. My brain told my mouth to use gentle words.

"Well, Buddy, there is something important for us to recognize. You are a highly gifted reader. It is rare to see someone your age read on your level. Very rare. I can see how you might think it's ordinary. You might think other kids can do it, too."

I took another breath. "But I have to tell you not everyone has your gift. Other kids have other strengths, different ways in which they excel, other ways in which they are extraordinary. But maybe reading is not one of them."

Buddy looked down and smiled. He absorbed the compliment, and he must have shared this exchange with his parents, though I'm not sure he absorbed the point I was trying to make.

Generally, Buddy was not a good listener. That was the heart of his problem. He called out comments throughout class, some germane to the topic at hand, some far afield. The worst ones inadvertently insulted other students. "Who doesn't know that?" he'd ask. He dismissed another kid's library selection as "This looks like a third-grade book."

We had been told that he was on medication for OCD and anxiety; he may also have been diagnosed on the autism spectrum, though we were not told that. He needed prompting sometimes and ignoring other times. He needed physical breaks from classwork to move about or take a walk down the hall. All of this was instituted and monitored in the most inconspicuous way because we were warned that it must never appear that he was being treated differently.

I got good at recognizing when his clear blue, excessively-focused eyes and his slightly rigid stature signaled he was ready to hijack the class with a filibuster on something like Egyptian hieroglyphics. Quickly I would block him, calling an end to class discussion and putting students in pairs or small groups for an exchange of ideas. Or I might assign journal writing or reading. Such defensive strategies saved me from having to wrest control once Buddy had seized the podium.

The good thing about Buddy was that he never exploded or cursed or bullied or intentionally hurt anyone. He just didn't know how to share the planet. What could we do in a class of 25 kids to help this boy join the human race? When I wondered whether the more experienced teachers were better qualified to handle Buddy than I was, they set me straight: We were all struggling.

Pressure from students like Buddy—and honestly, many others—did not help Donnell. Her patience was fraying like an old sweater. It took less and less to speed the unraveling.

Underneath her increasingly bellicose manner, Donnell had a great heart. I couldn't forget the times she had brought in shirts and sweatpants and even food for kids who had outgrown their clothes and clearly never got enough lunch. And there were the times when she insisted I join her on long drives to a hospital in another county where we watched our fragile student Elijah eventually disappear under the sheets plagued by a raging blood disease. The sight of him was almost unbearable, and yet I was so glad I had gone.

What became the last straw for Donnell developed so suddenly that when I went to find her after hearing about it her desk had already been cleared out.

The day it happened she was exhausted and the boy who challenged her was at his defiant worst. Exactly what happened—the boy was not physically harmed—was known only to the kids in her class, but as soon as they told it at home, Dave heard about it. He talked with Donnell, and she resigned on that cold day in February.

The whole thing made me so sad. I had come to love Donnell's gruffness if not some of her coarser language. While other teachers were busy being politically correct, she growled and groaned, expressing her real feelings. I knew I'd miss that rough-hewn frankness. A substitute took over her class, and I returned to mine feeling empty.

I needed to do something to lift my spirits. The good news was I could turn the dial. Each day brings new possibilities, especially in English class where a new act could always be written for our ongoing play. Lights. Camera. Action. It was February: Bring on the valentines!

I always loved Valentines Day. When I was a child, my siblings and parents and I filled a Valentine box with homemade creations bristling with rhymes and puns. At supper we handed them out, reading them aloud. One of my brothers designed paper catapults that launched accordion hearts when the card was opened.

I decided a valentine project for the class would lift me out of my funk. I worked my way around the natural awkwardness by turning l-o-v-e into a business proposition. I made up a story that a greeting card company was looking for fresh valentine messages and was sponsoring a contest for the best one.

"Really?" (Kids love contests.) "What's the prize?"

"Uh... candy!" (I had my basket of Jolly Ranchers standing by.)

Putting on a serious face, I explained the project, incorporating the grammar rules and literary devices of an exercise we needed to do anyway. Each valentine message had to contain at least one of the following: simile, metaphor, personification, hyperbole or onomatopoeia. Rhyme and meter could add great bounce—and maybe some extra credit.

After writing a few examples on the board (no one looked at them), I handed out lined paper and explained the protocol. First I had to approve their valentine message; only then could students get colored paper, glue and magazines to cut up and make their cards. We quickly reviewed what constituted a simile, a metaphor and the rest. Before setting them loose I said, "One final warning."

They all looked up. "Don't even try the 'roses are red, violets are blue' approach. The greeting card company won't touch those. Be creative! Be original!"

They got started, but it was a slow start and I began to hear grumbling.

"Who are these for, anyway?" Lindsey muttered.

"Do we have to say 'love'?" Cameron asked.

"This is so cheesy," Mac whined.

I strolled around the room. Cameron was typing into his phone.

"What are you doing?" I asked.

"Looking for pickup lines" he answered. I ignored him.

I was going to get fired up again. Maybe mere valentines might move kids toward a serious educational objective that some of us teachers had been working on. Student language was at the heart of a memo my colleague Anna and I had sent to the assistant superintendent the week before. To compose it, we stayed late one evening brainstorming ideas in a fevered session that was going so well we decided to record it.

"The level of language defines the level of thinking," one of us said.

"You can't think something you have no words for," the other said.

After I got home and described our lively conversation to my husband, he remembered a quotation about Abraham Lincoln and language. It came from a book Chris had read by Fred Kaplan, *Lincoln: The Biography of a Writer*. Kaplan wrote of Lincoln: "His was a personality and a career forged in the crucible of language." Imagine—a person, a life "forged in the crucible of language." And then this line blew my mind: "He became what his language made him." Absorbing this profound idea made me even more determined to make use of it.

Back in the classroom, only a few minutes had passed. Some students had begun to doodle time-worn rhymes on their papers before they remembered there would be no candy with that approach.

Eventually, they looked up and read the board, which had a handful of lines I'd saved, written by previous seventh graders:

"You are what happened when I wished upon a star," was one. And: "Falling in love is like throwing an interception."

Some kids began brainstorming in earnest and called me over for my opinion. Others had questions about whether their lines met the definition of one literary device or another. I could hear the buzz as the word-smithing took off.

Caleb was filling two sides of a sheet of folded paper with rhyming lines about how "Cupid is stupid. In a diaper, he's a love sniper." It was such a pleasure to see him jump to any task since Titanic had popped the cork on his spirit. He was having so much fun, I decided not to interrupt him. I moved on.

"What do you think of this? Is this good?" asked Mr. Bubbles, sporting a smile. "Your love is like WiFi, I can't live without it."

"Ah, combining a simile with hyperbole," I said, smiling back at him.

Hannah, who'd read her poem about divorce, wrote, "Your love makes me as dizzy as a roller-coaster."

"Voila! A simile wrapped together with some personification."

None of these would be going up on the board. But I loved the way kids were wrestling with high-density word packages. Wasn't this "the crucible of language"?

Chenlee carefully wrote the words love, family, China and teacher in the corners of her paper and drew arrows, stars and hearts of all sizes around the center. As I looked on, she was adding an American flag to the collage. She had come a long way since our only shared language had been that lovely paper bracelet.

Across the room of bent heads and scrawling pencils, I noticed Lance. He was not writing; he was snipping and folding paper. A few others noticed, too, yearning to pick up scissors rather than struggle with metaphors.

Before I could get aggravated, I reminded myself that mere participation was a victory for Lance the Bellman. I tried to look away and return my focus to what the rest of the kids were doing.

Lance had so much trouble with writing; even holding a pencil was hard. He also struggled with reading. Unless an adult was constantly at his side, he would fool around with another kid or wrap rubber bands around pencils, or doodle. Or he'd fold little pieces of paper—as he was doing now. Whenever I tried to steer him back to reading or writing he'd turn a stony face and clamp his jaw. Well, I consoled myself, now at least he was making a valentine.

Around the room, kids were delving into matters of the heart. I noticed the word love popping up here and there.

Some were stretching for creativity. I looked down at what Bronwyn was writing: "I don't care if it creates a parody, I don't care if you broke my trust, as long as you are standing here with me from the big bang to the end of the universe, I will do anything for you."

"Wow!" I said. "Talk about hyperbole!"

A few rows over, Hailey was challenging natural forces and not always getting the physics quite right: "You're my gravity, holding me up when I want to break down. You're the ground to catch me when I fall."

"Oh my, great metaphors and rhythm!" I gave her a thumbs-up, and she beamed.

Richard, a fast and natural writer, had finished building a message around an extended simile about "addicting love like a video game" and had gone on to shade in an edgy design.

"Can I do a second one?" he asked.

"Of course."

Finally, I announced a five-minute warning until cleanup time.

"Anyone who needs more time can finish their valentine tomorrow. And after that—we'll find out who the greeting card contest winners are."

Kids were reading their messages to each other and some were quietly asking me if they could keep theirs when it was over. It was hard not to smile, especially when I thought I knew which girl or boy they wanted to give it to.

Over by the wall, Lance was carefully taping the tips of purple, pink and white shapes together, alternating the colors. I had never seen him so absorbed. I was puzzled, fascinated. I stayed away so as not to disturb him, as you would with a rare bird at a feeder.

"Okay, all the paper on the floor must be picked up," I said. "Look under your chairs." They did.

I looked back over at Lance and finally saw what he was creating: an upright basket with scalloped hearts for sides and the base. It even had a handle.

Now, he was making a sort of swizzle stick by winding and twisting a piece of paper so tightly it was reduced to a very thin stalk. (For some reason I remembered a magic trick he once showed me with a paperclip, appearing at the tip of his finger and then disappearing.)

The bell was about to ring.

Lance was intently taping more hearts—this time only pink and white ones—in a gently overlapping circle to form a pinwheel. He attached it to the top of the purple swizzle stick to form a flower that went inside his heart basket. It was an engineering miracle and a paper magic trick. To my amazement, he then turned to a large purple heart and bent over it to write.

A purple heart, I thought. For a kid wounded in the combat of life.

The other kids gathered scraps for the trashcan and cardboard templates for the supply shelf. One by one, they turned in their valentine creations as the bell rang and they headed out, chatting and laughing.

Hurrying now, Lance taped a little hinged pink heart on the inside and wrote something under that. He folded the large purple heart closed. It would be the last thing to go in his basket. I walked over to him feeling sure he would ask to take the basket home. His mother would love it. But it saddened me to think the other kids wouldn't even see it.

He picked it up by the handle and held it out. The purple heart was addressed to me. "Read it," he said, pointing. His words celebrated the fun in our class, ending: "Every day, I say yay!"

The small pink heart had this message: "Open my heart." Inside, it said: "You are the key to my heart."

I looked at his shy smile and all I wanted to do was hug him. I resisted. Instead, covering my emotion I managed to mumble something about a great metaphor.

Lance was shimmering (or were those tears in my eyes?). He didn't speak, but he never stopped smiling.

We walked out together, me carrying the beautiful gift. Libby had just come out of her class when she spotted the heart basket and headed closer.

"Wow," she said, looking first at me then at him. "I believe design is in your future, Lance," she said, running her finger along the swizzle stick and then the flower. He looked down.

What might this paper valentine basket mean for this boy? Could it mark a new place in the classroom, and in the world?

"Open my heart," he had written. That was exactly what I had wanted to do all along.

# ELEVEN

# Perspective

Crossing the hall to my classroom, I caught a glimpse of Marianne around the edge of the counselor's door. Her eye makeup ran down her cheeks as she nodded at Mr. D's words. Then she bowed her head and her shoulders shuddered. He was leaning in, speaking very softly. I did a quick mental check of what I knew about Marianne's situation and came up clueless.

She had good grades, she had friends, she was considered popular. I couldn't visualize her as a victim. The big stress in her life that I knew about was her parents' divorce, but she seemed to be managing that pretty well.

Later that day, when I learned the cause of Marianne's heartache, I wanted to deny it. I wanted to roll back the tape and make it untrue. I wanted to offer her another moment before she made that bad decision. I wanted her to see that she had the power to decide against it.

Once again, I questioned myself. What could I do as a teacher?

Here's what happened. Marianne had gotten a text from an eighth-grade athlete who said he would be her boyfriend if she sent him a picture of herself topless.

At first his suggestion took her breath away, then shock and desire tumbled together in a roiling brew. The thought of going out with him, of cheering for him at games, of being his girl, excited her imagination like a fever.

Marianne pulled her best friend Alexa aside and showed her the text. Watching closely, Marianne could see the glint of jealousy brush across her friend's face before Alexa shook her head and shoved the phone away.

"Don't even think about it!" Alexa said. Sensing that her friend was considering it, she persisted: "Marianne! He's not worth it."

Yes, Marianne knew there was risk here, but she laughed and pretended only shock. Inside she felt the rush of the challenge. Such a catch. She went home to do her homework.

In her bedroom, with the door locked, she took off her top and then her bra. Flinging her long, blonde-streaked hair back over one shoulder, she took a selfie. Then several more. Within minutes, she picked the one that showed her smile in addition to what the eighth-grader wanted to see. She pressed "SEND".

As soon as he opened it, he showed it to four friends. They shared it, and other eighth-graders got a look. Soon a lot of seventh-graders would, too.

Hearing about this made me ponder my responsibility as a teacher. I couldn't have stopped that clock. I couldn't have contained that explosion. Nothing could. But again, what could I do?

One of the goals of any teacher is to help kids become critical thinkers, make smart decisions—question first before trusting and believing. As an English teacher, I had the golden opportunity to share literature with readers, encouraging them to freely judge characters and their motives, often harshly, because one could do that with fiction. All through a story or novel, I kept asking the class: Is this narrator or that character reliable or does he have a motive? Can we trust him? (Obviously, this exercise might have been useful in judging a popular athlete.)

I'd tell the kids: Think about a salesman or a politician who might say one thing to get another. Use a critical eye and a critical ear. Weigh all the evidence.

I'd tell them that back in my reporter days a healthy dose of skepticism was essential. One crusty editor's joking axiom about verification in every case: "If your mother says she loves you, check it out."

All through the year, we shared our own reactions to the literature we read. We also analyzed the craft of writing. Sometimes we focused on point of view. Critical thinking here: Every story presents a perspective, but is it the only one?

One experiment I set up pushed students to examine a common dilemma in fiction: Whom should I believe?

I told the class we would do an analysis of "Little Red Riding Hood." Of course, everyone groaned, thinking the text babyish and beneath them. Without letting on, I handed out two contradictory versions: Half the class got the traditional fairy tale while the other got a reworked version—the other side of the story—titled "The Maligned Wolf."

This second version told of a law-abiding wolf minding his own business and a spiteful little girl trespassing into his woods, picking flowers and littering food wrappers. The compassionate and civic-minded wolf tried to teach the girl a lesson only to be slandered and double-crossed by the selfish child.

Both halves of the class silently read their stories, but before our discussion would begin, I posed a few questions:

"Who is the hero? Who is the villain?"

"How do you know this? What convinced you?"

Confusion reigned. Those reading the familiar Brothers Grimm version were adamant: Red Riding Hood had been victimized. The other group was dumbfounded. How could their classmates fail to see the poor wolf's point of view? They used details from their story to make a case for the wolf. The Little Red Riding Hood defenders were aghast.

Preposterous! Where were these kids getting these crazy ideas?

That's when I stepped in to explain what was going on here: a lesson in perspective. We were examining two sides of what had seemed a simple story. We were showcasing the importance of questioning, doubting and proving.

Some kids wanted to expand our discussion into a formal, class-wide debate. Even better: Act it out in a courtroom.

"Let's have a trial!"

Sure. Why not? When a class erupts with that kind of energy it means the lesson goes to a new level, and I get to watch. I was delighted to let them be the drivers.

Kids spontaneously began moving desks, setting up the judge's bench, the witness stand, debating among themselves exactly how they wanted to reenact the scene.

Patricia, so often quiet, sad and disengaged, stepped forward with a gleam in her eyes. She had read the wolf's version.

"I want to prosecute Little Red Riding Hood," she announced. She didn't blink.

Oh dear, I thought. This was the same girl who continued to "forget" homework assignments and would shut down when I asked about her missing work. This was the girl whose father had confided that she'd given up on school and on herself. At times she displayed zero confidence.

Once when we were practicing argument-writing on the topic, "Will technology destroy or save civilization?" each student chose a side and wrote a claim. I recall Patricia, peering sadly at her computer screen. I pulled up a chair and offered to give her some feedback. Right away I could see that her setup was flawed: Two of her three supporting paragraphs relied on the same example.

"Let's combine these two paragraphs because they are both about education," I suggested with a bright voice.

"No, this one is about robots," she said.

"Yes," I said, "but it's about robots in education. It would fit neatly in the larger education paragraph and make it even richer." I smiled, trying to convey encouragement.

"No." She shook her head, stone-faced behind her glasses.

"What is it?" I asked. "What's wrong?" There may have been a bit of an edge in my voice.

She shook her head and wouldn't talk. I suggested we try to figure this out later, in study hall. But when she logged in then, her composition had disappeared—no content beyond the title.

"I don't know where it is," she said. I was certain she did know. She wouldn't look at me.

Here we were months later, ready to put Little Red Riding Hood on trial, and Patricia was intently watching me, waiting for a decision on whether she could have the prosecutor's role. Others were talking in small groups, brainstorming evidence and potential arguments. The energy level was high.

Kids had agreed on who would play the judge and jury. Cameron had persuaded everyone to let him be Little Red Riding Hood. I focused on Patricia. Could this girl possibly project the swagger of a prosecutor in this mock court of zealous, highly verbal classmates? She clearly wanted it. And this was the first time she'd shown that side of herself. I hated to say no.

"You want this role?" I asked her finally. "Okay."

Maybe she knew a thing or two about being misunderstood, like the wolf. Maybe, somehow, over the past few months she had started learning how to stand up for herself.

We quickly assembled the opposing sides of the case and reviewed everyone's roles. All the while I wondered if we would be witnessing a public humiliation for Patricia.

"All rise." The bailiff read the charges against Red Riding Hood:

"Unprovoked, malicious verbal attack and attempted murder of an innocent wolf." Patricia stood with her arms crossed, then paced as she waited for her opportunity to question the accused. She must watch *Law and Order*, I thought, holding my breath.

"Call the first witness." Cameron, with a flowered scarf on his head, came forward and everyone laughed.

Patricia silenced the room with a surprisingly loud and determined voice.

"You have alleged that the wolf approached you in the woods. Is that correct?"

Putting on a falsetto, Cameron piped, "Yes."

Unamused, Patricia continued. "Why were you trespassing on the wolf's property? Furthermore, why were you picking his flowers?"

Cameron began to protest, but Patricia raised her voice and spoke over him. "More importantly, why were you littering?"

Again, Cameron struggled to squeeze in an answer.

"You described the wolf as the aggressor!" Patricia challenged. Then, pointing directly at him, she added, "Isn't it quite clear here that you were the aggressor?"

Suddenly the girl I thought I had known was swept away. In her place stood an articulate, challenging lawyer with all the facts at her fingertips.

The "witness" faltered and seemed to grow smaller. Each time Cameron tried to defend his actions, Patricia shredded his arguments. She did the same with other witness "testimony" and gave a moving summation to the jury about the value of a good name. The greatest crime of all, she said, was staining the reputation of someone, even a wolf, branding him "big" and "bad" for all time.

"Guilty!"

Kerchiefed Cameron was led away to jail, defeated and perplexed—and loving the attention. Our "courtroom" erupted in cheers, the fairy tale turned on its head.

The bell rang. As students streamed out, I watched Patricia get her books.

"You were awesome," I said, still in a state of wonder. "Powerful."

"Thanks." Patricia flushed. Her smile, the first real one I'd seen in all the months I'd known her, completely changed her face.

I don't really know what happened there. Wallflower to prosecutor. Victim to conquerer. At the very least it seemed we had just witnessed a 13-year-old taking charge. It was something I wished Marianne had been able to do in a very different situation.

The forces that drive individuality run under the surface of each student, providing a strong, invisible power that I needed to recognize and encourage. Learning to stand up for oneself is a lifelong process, which requires examples, practice, opportunities.

By coincidence some colleagues and I had been shuttling back and forth to classes at Teacher's College at Columbia University in Manhattan, only a little more than an hour from our Connecticut town. We attended reading and writing workshops which espoused a teaching model based on the tenet that the student should be, to a great extent, in charge of his or her learning. The Columbia professors outlined ways to shift what they called "agency" from teacher to student. I looked up the word in Webster's. Agency: "The capacity, condition, or state of acting or of exerting power."

What if kids really did exert power over their own course of learning, making decisions and commitments on their own terms? What if they owned the process? Wasn't that exactly what happened during the impromptu trial I had just witnessed?

The magic of that moment when Patricia rose up and took over the class still gives me pause. But I suppose it shouldn't. Maybe it was just another seventh grade metamorphosis? The butterfly emerging, once again.

# TWELVE

# Being 13

As we approached the last lap of the school year, I took measure of the kids for the thousandth time. These weren't the ones who'd clambered noisily through my classroom door in the fall. It seemed indeed my cargo had changed. Snatches of overheard conversation now blossomed with opinions and insights that hadn't existed back in September. And boys and girls were noticing each other, reacting differently, blushing and stuttering sometimes. Very privately, Hannah asked me if I could change the seating chart to put her next to a special person. So many of my students were coming to the end of their larval stage; many now pushed at the edges of the chrysalis.

This was a time of new beginnings for us all. I remembered another springtime early in my teaching career, when I began making sense of new developments in my world. My mother had called to tell me that her cancer had returned; her doctor believed it had spread to her spine. Silence on my end of the phone. Three years earlier, when she told me about her initial diagnosis, I was flattened. Without breath. Frantic to help, to make it go away.

The intervening years had made me more logical, medical, strategic. "What's the protocol?" I asked her, refusing to let my voice shake.

I sensed we were in a losing situation. Time was speeding up—and my mother and father lived 1,000 miles away.

Springtime always finds me a bit vulnerable. It was in spring when our 16-year-old son left on a trip to Greece with a high school group. It was his first time so far away from home and that scared me. But this was something he had really wanted, and the trip ended up just fine. I needn't have worried so much. For me, spring was always about endings and beginnings.

One day after school, in the slanting sun of late afternoon, I watered our budding garden, flicking the hose over buttery daffodils and clumps of Russian irises. The glistening spray sparked flashes of brilliant light, like flickering frames in a movie reel. Blink and they're gone. It occurred to me that I had to keep my eyes wide open. Once again at that poignant time of year, I felt an urgency: about my mother before she died, about my son, and always about my students. I wanted them to take stock of who they were and where they were—how they were changing. Revelations seemed to come more frequently in class now, and I didn't want them to miss any. There was no time to waste.

I happened to be reading *Gilead*, the eloquent and moving novel by Marilynne Robinson, in which the narrator is an aging minister who knows he hasn't long to live. He grieves about the prospect of abandoning his young son and uses this to shape a sermon that cites the Old Testament story of Abraham sending his son Ishmael into the wilderness because God commanded him.

How could God do that? The rhetorical question led the minister to reveal his epiphany. Fixing an eye on his congregation, he reminded them that we are "made instruments of His providence"—after all, God is in the wilderness, too. The reader senses he's also reminding himself.

Like that fictional sermon-giver, I want to share some of my epiphanies with my students. I'm sure many teachers are like me. When realization explodes in front of us, we bring it into the classroom.

It is my habit to lightly weave poetry through the course of the year. In springtime, however, I start a sustained and pretty rigorous poetry unit, simply because I believe that carefully selected poems offer kids a lens to take a closer look at themselves.

This year, I began reading aloud to the class Mary Oliver's poem, "The Journey." It opens with these lines:

> *One day you finally knew*
> *what you had to do, and began,*
> *though the voices around you*
> *kept shouting*
> *their bad advice—*

I glanced up. The faces in front of me showed I had their attention. I continued reading—about leaving old voices behind, hearing your own voice and striding onward,

> *determined to do*
> *the only thing you could do—*
> *determined to save*
> *the only life you could save.*

Those last words seemed to hang in the still air. "…the only thing… the only life…" The kids were struck silent, riveted. This was not what I would have seen at the beginning of the year.

We began to decode each line, even each word, with kids writing in the margins on their copies, me on the board. In this free-form search for meaning, there was comfort in numbers, in the shared insights emerging in our dense notations. We concluded that the poet was finding herself, clawing her way toward honesty and individuality.

On the board, I wrote a quote from another poet, E.E. Cummings, and invited students to reflect on how this bit of prose related to Oliver's poem:

"To be nobody but yourself in a world which is doing its very best day and night to make you like everybody else means to fight the hardest battle which any human being can fight and never stop fighting."

After reading it aloud, I moved over to the big window and looked down at the woods glowing in the bright green of new growth.

"Why is being yourself such a hard job?" I asked. "Cummings uses the word fight, and we know poets choose words carefully. Why does he use that word?"

Richard, who knew what fighting for yourself meant, went first.

"Simple," he said. "It's much easier for the world if everyone is alike and predictable. It's like a force you have to fight."

Bronwyn raised her hand. "It is harder to be different than it is to go along," she said. "But it is also true that most people have a strong desire to fit in."

We moved on to a reading of Langston Hughes' poem, "Mother to Son," in which a woman exhorts her son to "keep climbing" because life for her, she says, "ain't been no crystal stair."

I asked the class: How many of your parents made it clear that you would not always succeed, that you would sometimes struggle, that life was no "crystal stair"?

Bailey's hand shot up. This quiet girl had not shared much in class discussion, but she had written a lot in her journal about troubles at home. Kids turned with a curious interest.

"When was that, Bailey?" I asked.

She let out a puff of exasperation. "In fifth grade. When everything in my family got messed up and we had a talk."

"What did you learn?"

Bailey shifted in her seat and hesitated a moment. "I learned that stuff you depend on doesn't always work out. Families don't stay together." She looked down. "Parents aren't always honest. Stuff like that."

She spoke with the authority of a survivor.

Then a question from Bronwyn, directed at me:

"What did you tell your children?" Her tone was not mocking, of course, but just curious. Without missing a beat, I answered:

"I told my son that life would be great and he would shine."

Her eyes didn't leave my face.

"And then?"

"Well, then I had to make excuses or suggest other plans, like 'you'll get on another team,' or 'there are other people to be friends with.'" She smiled.

"You get the picture," I continued. "You know what I should have said?"

Cameron blurted: "Life ain't a crystal stair."

Richard corrected: "Ain't NO crystal stair."

As kids laughed, I said, "Yeah, you're probably right," then asked what they imagined they'd tell their own children. Crystal stair, or not?

Other poems took us down these winding paths; besides analyzing meaning we paid attention to how the music of poetry works. Meter, rhythm and rhyme filled our ears. We considered the impact of the perfectly chosen word.

Then I announced their new assignment:

"Your job is to choose a poem to memorize and recite in a couple of weeks."

"I can't do that!" Bailey wailed. A chorus of groans agreed.

"Why can't we just pick one and read it?" Cameron pleaded.

I was ready for the pushback. "The only way to really get inside a poem, to know it inch-by-inch, is to memorize it," I said. More groans. "You are all going to surprise yourselves—you will gain composure and confidence from this. You'll be able to do it."

I had carefully prepared a list of poets and websites to help students find a poem that was meaningful to them.

My deadline for selections arrived, and the kids came to class with printed pages. As I approved titles, I noticed some surprises. Once-meek Patricia chose a strident poem by Maya Angelou; Richard, who had often tried to keep things simple, submitted an intricate Shakespeare sonnet; ball-playing Jack O'Hara picked a poem about war.

By strange coincidence, while we were reviewing their choices, a former student, then in eighth grade, came into the classroom to ask me for help with a newspaper article he was working on. (I was the advisor to the school paper).

As he watched, I asked students who had already started memorizing to recite their first line when I pointed to them. I felt like an orchestra conductor, pointing this way and that, hearing not musical notes but the words of Emily Dickinson, John Keats and finally Richard's Shakespeare:

> *Shall I compare thee to a summer's day?*
> *Thou art more lovely and more temperate…*

Without a pause, our visiting eighth-grader spoke the next lines:

> *Rough winds do shake the darling buds of May,*
> *And summer's lease hath all too short a date…*

He continued reciting all the way to the sonnet's end.

"See guys," I said to the open-mouthed rows of kids, "that's going to be you in about a week."

I continued logging in titles, leaving Amir for last, because I guessed he hadn't chosen one. For although he was now contributing to the class in many ways, I anticipated this assignment might be too big a leap for him. I approached his desk. "How about you, Amir?"

He shrugged.

I handed him what has long been a favorite poem of mine, one that I thought might work. It was Robert Frost's, "Acquainted With The Night."

> *I have been one acquainted with the night.*
> *I have walked out in rain—and back in rain...*

Reading it over, Amir slowly nodded.

The initial class-wide resistance to my memorization assignment gradually yielded to mere reluctance, then to a real enthusiasm. Kids began reciting between classes, folding and unfolding their copies as they tested themselves. In class, they paired off to practice.

Leaning against the lockers in the back of the room, Logan began his choice, "Ozymandias" by Percy Bysshe Shelley:

> *I met a traveler from an antique land,*
> *who said: 'Two vast and trunkless legs of stone*
> *stand in the desert'...*

His partner, Seth, gave him a thumbs up and took his turn with one by Emily Dickinson, a subtle lament about approaching death:

> *I have not told my garden yet,*
> *Lest that should conquer me:*
> *I have not quite the...*

He scratched his head.

"Strength." Logan cued.

"Yeah, yeah," Seth said, continuing:

> *...strength now*
> *To break it to the bee.*

All around the room kids were holding poems while their partners recited, eyes locked together. Prompts and corrections were quick and polite but relentless. No errors: That was the standard. Some recited into recording apps on their phones. Some asked me to listen.

Cameron pulled me aside; he wanted to go out in the hall so I could hear his. He said he was afraid someone might distract him. At first I was disappointed to see that he had chosen "The Unwritten," by W. S. Merwin, a poem we had already thoroughly deconstructed in class. It seemed the short-cut artist within Cameron remained alive and well. But then, in the hall, he trembled as he stumbled along, line by line, staring at me for support.

> *Inside this pencil*
> *crouch words that have never been written*

He squinted, trying to remember.

> *never been spoken,*
> *never...*

He searched for the words.

> *...been taught.*

He paused. Covered his face.

> *...they're hiding*
> *they're awake in there...*
> *dark in the dark...*

He stopped, shaking his head and looking defeated.
"Oh. I forget the next line."

I patted him gently on the shoulder.

"That was a wonderful start," I said. "It almost seems like you are speaking your own words—ideas you have stored inside."

"I'll get this," he said, standing straight again. "I'll get this."

His transformation moved me. For once, he wasn't just bucking for a good grade. Instead, he seemed to be taking measure of his unwritten self. I hadn't seen this coming.

"Life can only be understood backwards, but it must be lived forwards," the philosopher Soren Kierkegaard wrote a couple of hundred years ago. (I had put this quote on the board months before as a writing prompt. Now I applied it to myself.) I guess I would have to wait to really understand some things. I thought of another quote I'd used, also as a writing prompt: "A mind that is stretched by new experience can never go back to its old dimensions." That was Oliver Wendell Holmes, Jr.

Cameron had been stretched. And of course he wasn't alone.

One day, I loaned my phone to Jack O'Hara, who was practicing "In Flanders Fields" by John McCrae. I had activated the recording app for him and stood nearby. Later, I replayed that two-minute recording. The juxtaposition of Jack's voice and the poet's words electrified me. This 13-year-old boy who once seemed to love only baseball now spoke with a huskiness and a quivering nervousness about the row on row of crosses in a World War I cemetery where poppies grow. About larks flying above. About guns echoing below.

*We are the dead...*

He paused.

*Short days ago*
*we lived, felt dawn, saw sunset glow...*

The voice was so young, the story no longer old. The graves were fresh again. As McCrae's words unfolded, it sounded as if Jack was taking in a new understanding. He had expected heroics from a poem about war, but his focus had shifted, during the rereading and memorizing, from battlefield to graveyard. Was losing sight of sunset glow worth it? There were no living soldiers on Flanders Field in that scene, just the quandaries of war.

Finally the day for public recitations arrived. Students settled into their desks, murmuring, holding accordioned scraps of paper that contained the stanzas they hoped they'd remember. The air was electric.

Patricia, who had broken free as our class prosecutor, wanted to go first.

"My poem is 'Still I Rise,' by Maya Angelou," she said, standing at the podium, proudly empty-handed. Head erect, eyes locked on the back bookcase, she began:

> *You may write me down in history*
> *With your bitter, twisted lies,*
> *You may trod me in the very dirt*
> *But still, like dust, I'll rise…*

She seemed to rise herself. A phoenix.

Next came Bronwyn's turn. Without consulting her note cards, she recited the 32 lines of Rudyard Kipling's timeless poem "If," which includes:

> *If you can trust yourself*
> *when all men doubt you,*
> *But make allowance for*
> *their doubting too…*

The seventh-grade "spy," Lara, recited "The Tyger" by William Blake, ending with a remarkable command in her voice:

*What immortal hand or eye*
*Dare frame thy fearful symmetry?*

The kids watched each other with fascination, but the intensity was getting to me. Then Amir stepped forward. He smoothed the paper copy I had given him and, before saying anything, just looked around at his classmates. He had not memorized his poem, I knew. But I was not sure what would happen next. Would he start with a complaint about the assignment itself, or even the pointlessness of memorization?

Nothing like that.

"My poem is called 'Acquainted with the Night.' It's by Robert Frost," he said. Then, looking up from time to time, he read about darkness and "walking out in rain." His voice, speaking adult truths, was distant and raw.

*I have outwalked the furthest city light*
*I have looked down the saddest city lane...*

Staring at him, I wondered: What night was in the mind of this troubled son of a bitter single mother, with whom he did puzzles for comfort?

*I have passed by the watchman on his beat*
*And dropped my eyes, unwilling to explain...*

Row by row, students sat hushed, wrapped in the despair of Amir's new/old voice. When he finished, there were none of the usual cheers. The room was intensely quiet. Finally, breaking the silence, Cameron asked: "How did you make it sound so real?"

Slowly, Amir spoke. "I live this, that's how," he said. "This is my life."

That night I called my sister Ellen to tell her about my day. I described Amir's reading and wondered if I had unintentionally increased the loneliness he felt by giving him that Frost poem.

"Oh, no, just the opposite," she answered with the thoughtful voice she used in her yoga classes. "When we can see a connection between something in the outside world and some essential part of ourselves, it gives us strength. It builds a foundation of truth within us. What is heartbreaking is that it took all this time for someone to bring it to this young person. Don't you think?"

She was right. Although I couldn't change Amir's situation, I could offer up Robert Frost to join him on those dark streets.

I did sometimes worry I might be asking too much of 13-year-olds. Was I rushing their maturity when I asked them to scale the heights of these poems, with their steep, jagged, grown-up truths? Were my kids ready?

There was one thing I did know they were ready for. So many had asked from the beginning, "Can't we write our own poems?" Finally, it was time. Their poems would be experiments in introspection. But there was a major stipulation: I would give them the topic. I even assigned the title: "Being 13."

The words were barely out of my mouth when Mae cried out, "I'm not 13 yet."

"I don't get it," Richard said, ignoring Mae, but puzzled by the title I was insisting on.

I kept going. "If you aren't 13 quite yet, you can write about what you anticipate 13 will be like."

"Pretty much like 12," murmured Logan, not quite under his breath.

That brought an instant reaction from Seth, who turned in his seat to look at Logan, hunched behind him.

"Are you kidding me!?"

We started by brainstorming what it meant to be 13. As students volunteered ideas from their own experience, I wrote them down on a giant chart propped on an easel at the front of the class.

"There is so much pressure on me now," Lindsey said. "When I was 12 nobody even noticed me. I could do anything I wanted. Now I have so much more responsibility." Of course, since she lost her older sister, she must have started taking on the role of oldest as well.

I wrote "pressure" and "responsibility" on the chart. It soon filled up: "Mood swings. Freedom. Chores. Changes. Labeling. Boyfriends. Popularity. Loss of childhood. Judgment. Depression. Exciting. Lost. Alone. Fake friends. Drama!! Stuck in-between. Puberty. Trying to belong. Independent. Misunderstood. Choices. Unique. Being yourself. Reputation."

Thirteen was everything from "Love" to "Pimples."

In the following days, kids made their own organizers. They drew large graphic outlines of the numerals 1 and 3 and filled them with words from the chart that reflected their own experiences. Next, they began expanding the message into a poem. Some of their lines of verse sparkled:

> *There's so much to dream at night,*
> *just close your bright eyes,*
> *and step into the sunlight,*
> *you're only thirteen,*
> *you're going to be alright.*

Others hinted at social awkwardness:

> *If 12 is Disney World, 13 is Las Vegas*
> *Straight hair*
> *wrong shoes*
> *lip gloss*

*how to kiss?*

There was pain in some, but hope peeked out:

> *I imagine*
> *the opportunity to discover*
> *strength*
> *to fix the broken me…*

Poems-in-progress were shared for feedback. Kids traded advice, rewrote, polished.

All in preparation for the final—and scariest—part of the assignment: Presenting their original poems in a grade-wide assembly. This would be their D-Day. I told them that if presenting alone on the stage was too terrifying, they could form pairs or small groups. Some leapt at that chance.

On the morning of the assembly the whole seventh grade—all of my classes and all of Shannon's—filled the lunchroom: about 250 kids sitting cross-legged in rows on the floor. House lights went down, stage lights beamed, microphones went live. All the seventh-grade teachers—math, science, social studies, Spanish lined the walls to hear their kids open up. The show began.

One class at a time, students lined up backstage by the steps, waiting for their turn to take the mic and read.

"I think I'm going to throw up," one whispered.

"I can't do this," another insisted.

"I have to go to the bathroom," someone moaned.

They were pacing, praying, hyperventilating.

"You'll be fine," I kept telling them, like a doctor before giving a shot. "It'll be over quickly."

From the steps, we listened to one amplified voice after another, punctuated by applause, as kids yielded the mic to the next in line. We watched them come back down the stairs, faces flushed and covered in smiles, as their hands shot up for high-fives.

"OMG. I did it!" they would cry out in an explosive whisper, before rejoining the audience on the other side of the curtain.

Many of these kids had never been so scared and never felt so proud just a few minutes later. It was a fiery challenge, yet they all survived. On top of all that, some were sharing deep, personal feelings.

Bailey, who'd learned early that life was no crystal stair, began with the analogy of 13 as "always an ocean," and added:

> *Waves of emotion overwhelm me*
> *mermaids laugh as they swim by.*
> *A mermaid I will never be.*

Oh. To accept that fate at age 13? I'd read her words earlier, of course, but now she was saying them out loud. They brought back some old, sad lines from Thomas Gray's poem, "Elegy Written in a Country Church-Yard":

> *Full many a flower is born to blush unseen...*

"Unseen."

"A mermaid I will never be."

I'd talk to Bailey.

The recitations went on, full of epiphanies bravely shared.

One was a remarkable presentation by a deep-voiced, downcast boy hardly any of us knew. He and a small group of other kids spent the whole day in a single classroom designed for the most emotionally challenged seventh graders. His poem described the student "no one cares about."

> *As a kid I went through some personal stuff*

*But all I'm going to say is that it was tough...*

He spoke about himself as an outsider, listening and watching others laugh and jostle together, while he remained "invisible" on the sidelines. He ended with:

> *So, don't take this to heart*
> *And after this don't clap*

But of course, the astonished lunchroom did explode with applause before he disappeared into the wings as mysteriously as he had arrived. In between, he'd declared his truth about "Being 13."

# THIRTEEN

# Remember Me

The end of the school year was only two weeks away. Five seventh-grade teachers lounged in a friendly circle, meeting for the last time. Our agenda was simply to decide the activities for field day, coming up soon.

One thing was quickly agreed: No ice pops. That was easy after the previous year's sticky debacle of impenetrable wrappers that—once scissors were found—littered the ground everywhere. Another easy one: No water-balloon toss. With his usual directness, Ben nixed that: "Boys will throw them at girls."

We settled on tug-of-war and some kind of ball game. And, what else? We were narrowing safe options when there was a quick knock on the door. It was Bud, our burly assistant principal, towering in the doorway, grinning.

"Look what I found," he said, sure we'd share his joy as he stepped aside to reveal the familiar face of a blonde girl, now 18, wearing dark eye makeup and dangling earrings. We all remembered Kira.

Students do come back. Sometimes it's for approval, forgiveness, reconnection, praise. Or just to see how small their old desks look. Sometimes, kids like Kira return to see the teachers who believed in them and stood in for harried or absent parents.

These were the teachers who added them to a lunch-bunch group, welcomed them into after-school clubs, nudged them towards sports teams, or, as we'd done with Kira—how many times?—urged good books over bad boys. Every one of her small successes won praise from us. We had cradled Kira. And now here she stood, two weeks before high-school graduation, holding a tiny bundle in a baby blanket.

My eyes flicked to Libby's, and I realized we had the same thought. Oh, no. We lost this one.

Still, we stood and cooed and beamed at the little one—and told Kira, as she left, to stay in touch.

Visits weren't always as complicated—or bittersweet. Some kids seem to return mainly to show us that our investment had paid off.

A few months earlier, a former student named Emily floated back after 12 years, ostensibly to see her little brother in my English class. She was now a TV anchor on early-morning news in a small city out west. Standing before my seventh graders, she was a star. She pointed to one of the desks.

"I sat there," she said. The current occupant tapped his finger tips on the desktop, absorbing the magic—and making Emily smile at a sudden memory. Turning to me, she said, "Thank you, by the way, for putting up with my desk drumming." I winked at her. Emily had been one of those kids who had to keep moving, and with her it resulted in a constant, edge-of-desk drumroll.

"I wasn't a very good student," she confessed to the class, "but I remember seventh grade so clearly—my locker, my friends. I even remember the poem I memorized. Do you guys have to memorize a poem?"

"Oh, yeah!" They answered in unison. One voice rose over the others. "I bet you can't recite yours." It was Cameron, of course.

"Want to hear it?" she teased. Then, in her broadcaster voice, she launched into "The Walrus and the Carpenter," Lewis Carroll's non-sense poem.

Yes, they do come back.

All too quickly, the last full day of school arrived. I always hated the end. It sounds nonsensical, but I was plagued by the notion that I wasn't finished. I remembered Pat Conroy, the great novelist who started out as a teacher, comparing graduation to "the end of a small civilization." I knew he was right. I wasn't ready for them to go and for all traces of our little civilization to disappear. All the same, they were leaving.

And so was I. After 13 years of teaching I had decided to retire.

For me there wouldn't be another batch of seventh graders next fall. I had found it very hard to announce this news to the kids and so had put it off until the final week. This is how it went: I called my first class to attention.

"I have an announcement to make." A little throat-clearing. "This will be my last year as a teacher here." Silence. "I'm retiring."

Empty, uncomprehending faces stared at me after I said these words, which seemed to have landed like the thud of a badly planned lesson.

"Why?" The voice was soft, almost a whisper.

It was a logical question. Suddenly my departure felt a bit like a betrayal. We had been in this relationship together. Why would I call it quits? Why was I leaving?

I stumbled at first. I hadn't anticipated how hard it would be to explain. Vaguely I talked about plans to write and travel, but couldn't adequately account for my departure in terms that my students could understand.

Of course, I would never say that the early mornings and long, working weekends with towering stacks of papers to grade had taken a toll. I didn't want to acknowledge I was getting tired as I hit my mid-60s, that I wanted to go out at the top of my game. Not like some.

It had been a brilliant run, but it was time for my husband and me to fold up our tents and move into the third act of our lives.

All the same, I didn't want to just go. Partly to slow time, partly to ritualize the end, I had planned a ceremony for the kids in my last homeroom. I wanted to honor each quirky personality with a symbolic gift.

Going through my closets and cupboards, I found so many items that had been used in class—gimmicks and gizmos, props for writing prompts. These mementoes could become awards of a kind. A rainmaker and a rhythm shaker that I had used for sound effects during dramatic readings. A stained-glass star suctioned to my big window. A silver bell, a hacky sack. Origami, Play-Doh, wind-up toys, stuffed animals, rock 'n' roll CDs (played when we read a novel set during the Vietnam War). As I sifted, I waited for inspiration to strike.

When I couldn't find the right item for a particular kid, I put another name on my list for a shopping spree at the Dollar Store.

As I mentally linked objects with students, the ceremony took shape. Unearthed from the back of a shelf, I pulled out candy-colored lights used years before—I can't remember why—and ran them along the top of the white board, making a perfectly ridiculous backdrop for the "show."

All 22 homeroom students returned from lunch that day for study hall, tumbling back into their seats, snatching each other's water bottles, calling out and generally creating a squall of noise. I flipped the gaudy lights on and announced that I needed their attention.

"It's Awards Day!"

Total focus.

The first award was something I'd bought for Logan, the boy who'd told me he had no friends. Earlier that day, he had said he wasn't coming to our afternoon study hall, and didn't care about the "awards." We'd made a deal that he would come for just a minute and I would present to him first.

It happened that, from time to time throughout the year, Logan had written unassigned poems and placed them by my laptop. They referenced concepts like eternity and anonymity. One poem had a line about "God's unedited notebook" in which we are all mentioned.

That poem showed promise, as did some others, and I wanted him to realize that. But each time I tried to compliment him, he ducked away and disappeared. So for his end-of-year award, I copied one of his poems and taped it into a journal with gilt-edged pages. I presented it to "the poet laureate of our homeroom." He received the book, opened it and sat motionless, head tilted down as if he didn't know exactly what to do.

The second prize needs a bit of explanation. It was a busted baseball; its horsehide exterior had split open at a seam, no doubt due to some long-ago crack of the bat. The minute I picked it up from a patch of grass while on a walk past a baseball diamond in our town park, I imagined a future writing assignment for the class: "Tell the story of what happened during this last game—from the ball's perspective."

Naturally, this award went to Jack O'Hara, who had found the courage to tell his football-coaching father that he loved baseball instead.

"This is what happens to a ball when Jack hits it," I announced grandly. Everyone hooted as he came forward to claim it.

For helping me run the class, design seating charts, organize the student supply area, advise me on various high-level matters, Juliana was awarded a fitting prize, the silver bell I had used to quiet the class.

A fat pack of brilliantly colored origami papers went to Chenlee to replenish the steady supply of handmade gifts she fashioned and handed out in all directions. She went to work immediately with a silver sheet I guessed might be a thank-you gift for me.

I called Bailey forward and pressed a *Little Mermaid* cake ornament into her hand (Dollar Store). I didn't mention her verse declaring, "a mermaid I will never be." Nor did I have to. She touched the curving tail and closed her hand around it.

Chaz, who dreamed of making the Olympic swimming team, and had responded instantly to my "teacher-equals-coach" talk early in the year, got a large foam noodle (Dollar Store again) because "even champions need to take a rest sometimes." He grinned as wide as his wingspan.

At this point the students were quieting each other, eager to know what was coming.

It was time for Bronwyn. She got the blue, red, yellow and green stained-glass star from the window. "This signifies the light Bronwyn reflected on us all year. Like a star's light," I said.

I glanced over her head and out the window to the view that had led me through 13 lucky years. It had shifted month by month—from the cloudless Indian summer sky that drew the eyes of new and uncertain students, to the painted leaves of autumn, then to the black-and-white of the snowy woods studded with bare trees, soon to become green buds of spring, and finally to almost-summer and butterflies. I pulled myself back into the room to take in all the transformation that had occurred here, inside. Here they were, my butterflies.

It was time for an oversized jar of "Aegean Blue" bubble solution (wand attached). Eyes crinkled around the room; everyone knew who would get that.

"Mr. Bubbles!" my voice boomed. Alexander, who stood taller than me now, strode past the desks to the front of the room as if accepting an Oscar. He turned to face the class holding the jar, ducked his head and began to giggle. Everyone clapped as he stumbled back to his desk.

The next award, found in an old-fashioned variety store, was a plastic rotary phone that might have suited an oversized dollhouse. I pulled it up onto the lectern and pantomimed getting a call, head tilted, receiver on my ear.

"Oh," I said looking up in feigned surprise as if I'd forgotten the kids were there. "They're asking for you, Hailey." I gestured for her to come forward.

"This is a backup just in case someone takes your cell phone." Hailey was mesmerized by the rotary dial that actually moved.

"So retro," she crooned and began making "calls" immediately.

Lance, the master crafter whose valentine had stolen my heart (and still sits on a shelf at home), got a rainbow collection of construction paper. He was quiet, almost formal, as he came forward to accept his award. I never knew what went on in that head of his.

Richard—the writer, the survivor of a lost father, and a fanatic about root words and derivations—got a book of advanced crossword puzzles to keep him busy all summer.

"I didn't have the heart to give you a book on punctuation," I said, grinning.

I held up a glittery red-white-and-blue top hat (yes, Dollar Store). "Citizen of the year!" I said, pointing to Cameron who had turned into someone I could admire. Of course, he rushed forward, put it on and proceeded to march around the desks using his pencil as a baton.

My eyes fell on Seth. His mellow slouch had not changed during these often raucous presentations. He looked bemused. Time for another hand-me-down—my own Starbucks coffee cup.

"Seth, this will help you stay awake in English class next year," I said, raising the mug in a toast as he slowly unfolded himself and sauntered to the podium to take it by the handle. A George Clooney smile slowly spread across his face.

"You always get it right," he said, shaking his curly mop of hair.

Just three prizes left. The one for Lindsey had taken me a while to figure out. She had come through a very hard year, losing a sister. And she had discarded the too-cool-for-school attitude. Rummaging through my shelves, I'd found a kaleidoscope that seemed fitting. I dedicated it to Lindsey "for finding light even in the darkness—turning the lens to the color." She thanked me and slowly rotated the glass-filled cap, creating one bright mosaic after another.

If Bronwyn had been the conscience of our class, Hannah had been its bravest member. What could I give her? Nothing in the closet was quite right. And then it popped up in my jewelry box at home, of all places. I don't remember where it came from. It was a round bronze-like medal suspended from a folded ribbon, featuring the profile of a figure wearing a short hat. I called it a "medal for bravery" when I called her forward.

"Why? What for?" she asked.

"You led the way when you read your poem last fall about your 'two worlds'. That was long before anyone could imagine such courage," I said, thanking her.

The last item on the shelf below the podium was a box with a puzzle in it. I lifted it up for all to see.

"Amir is the recipient of this puzzle because he understands so many of the pieces that go into the big picture of life," I said, "and because he knows how to put this challenging thing together."

He sat close enough to receive the box without rising as I extended it to him. He nodded, looking straight at me. He and I both knew the value of the time we had spent together, working side-by-side. That seemed like a century ago, in a different place and time. (Later, I would get an email with thanks and, "This is just to let you know I'm not as angry.")

When it was all over, I "raffled" off a few CDs and we played a little of each one. The enthusiasm was high—greatly disproportionate to the quality of the music.

It was time for the bell, and Logan, who hadn't wanted to come, was still sitting in the front row—with his hand on his book of golden-edged pages.

After my homeroom students left, there were a few more classes before the final bell of the year. In each of these, as in my morning classes,

I asked kids to read back through their journals and talk about how they saw themselves differently now.

"How have you changed?" was my question. Some classes had become so much like family that kids actually talked frankly, even bluntly, like siblings about how much each other had grown.

I wondered who would start. To my surprise it was the bright but contained mermaid Bailey. (She, like all my homeroom students, was also in one of my English classes). Her eyes landed on a boy halfway across the room, causing both of them to smile.

"Patrick has become more serious," she said. "He's not always starting arguments." It was true. In the beginning, "Patrick Henry" had held back his feelings during class discussions, relying instead on mildly sarcastic—and, yes, funny—side-comments. I knew from his journal-writing that he had a deep, serious side. I heard the warmth in Bailey's voice. Patrick blushed but didn't crack a joke.

Lindsey jumped in at this point, gesturing toward a stern face in the front row. "Amir has really become part of the class," she said, then asked if I agreed.

"Yes," I said. "He has." I nodded at his serious expression, knowing there was much more going on in his heart than his face ever showed. The fact is, the others felt he was beginning to belong. I really believed he felt that too, for the first time.

Bronwyn raised her hand to talk about her feelings for the class as a whole.

"It's funny," she said. "I've never been so comfortable in a class. In fact, I'm more myself than I have ever been—and you guys know I'm a little different—a bit too crazy about environmental issues and other stuff."

When she added, "But you've all been nice to me," there was a low and friendly cluck of support from kids sitting all around her. Then Bronwyn's wire rims focused squarely on me. "I hope you won't forget us," she said.

In a sliver of a moment I was transported back to James Hilton's famous character "Mr. Chips." In the last month of his life, the fictional English schoolmaster, drifting mentally and picturing the faces of the hundreds of boys he had taught, addressed those who doubted he'd remember them: "But I do remember you—as you are now. That's the point. In my mind you never grew up at all. Never."

Hilton wrote *Goodbye, Mr. Chips*, based on his own schoolmaster father and other teachers he had known. Tenderly, he described the world they all inhabited: "School days are a microcosm of life—the boy is born the day he enters school and dies the day he leaves it…But outside this cycle stands the schoolmaster, remembering faces and incidents as a god might remember history."

Bronwyn couldn't have known how deeply my time with her and the others would be engraved on my memory. I also heard something she didn't even say. I heard the universal desire for connection from 13-year-olds who had become individuals on my watch. I heard a wish to be recognized, to matter.

"How could I forget about you?" I said, turning to Bronwyn.

A sudden shout: "Wait a minute! What about me?"

"Cameron!? You!? You almost killed me," I shouted back. "How could I forget that? I have the scars." I let out a laugh.

On that last day, kids wrote farewell notes on the whiteboard. They remembered silly things we had done like a spontaneous dance contest. One suggested I change my mind and teach them again in eighth grade. Caleb signed his note, "John Jacob Astor" from the Titanic.

And one wrote simply: "Now I love to write!"

My heart thumped a little harder. Take that love out the door into another grade, into another world, I thought.

Another board note: "How will you survive without me?"

God, I loved that one. The shiny self-confidence of a child-turning-adult made me laugh out loud. So personal. So saucy.

The dismissal bell signaled that the buses would line up for the last time that school year and the doors would burst open, releasing torrents of kids heading home. Some flung their arms around me, others stood teary-eyed.

Then they were gone.

Teachers, aides, nurses, counselors, administrators and office workers all hurried down the hallways to gather on the little patch of grass in front of the school to wave as the buses took our kids away for summer.

Libby and I met Deborah at the exit. We knew Donnell wouldn't be there. Neither would Henry Curry, who had particularly liked this tradition. The buses lined up like elephants, head to tail, around the circular drive in front of the school. I searched for Anna in the throng of teachers and found her surrounded by her sixth-grade colleagues. We shared a bittersweet grin.

All of the bus windows were half-open and filled with the faces of kids shouting goodbyes as the drivers leaned on their horns. We waved our arms over our heads and chorused the classic *Nah Nah Nah Nah, Nah Nah Nah Nah, Hey Hey Hey, Goodbye*—until the last exhaust pipe rounded the corner of the street and it was just us grownups.

"Congratulate yourselves," one teacher called out. "We survived Jimmy Grady."

"I know which ones I won't miss," Ally deadpanned.

We trooped back into the now-silent building to pack up our rooms, humming with plans for the summer break until that first meeting in late August renewed the cycle of a new school year. Except, not for me.

For me, packing up was always an existential experience, especially so in this final school year. People talk about what happens to students. What about us? What about the teachers who are left trembling with the knowledge that something profound has occurred in littered rooms with desks out of line and chairs askew?

Evidence of the mountaintop climb the kids and I had shared was everywhere in my sunny room; I was left at base camp, breathless, taking in the view. Outside that window, the one we had all been drawn to, lay their future.

I turned to the baskets that held some left-behind journals (I had persuaded most kids to take them home and keep them forever) and flipped through one, noticing for the first time that Mr. Bubbles described himself as intensely shy on his first page of writing. That was why he seemed so expressionless, maybe. Thank God for the laughter. I put the notebook back and started to walk my room one last time.

At the bulletin board I read samples of student reflections on a project after it was done.

Here and there I came upon posted book reviews, files of detention notes and grade sheet printouts—all now seeming like the layers of an archeological dig taking me back in time to where it had all begun. When I thumbed through my copy of our yearbook my eyes fell on a note from Gabrielle, the girl who'd beheaded her sister's doll: "Thank you for listening to me when I needed someone to talk to."

As the afternoon passed, Libby, Deborah, Anna and others dropped in to give me a goodbye hug. I knew I'd see some of them for coffee or a glass of wine in the future, but we would never again be in the trenches together.

I came upon a pile of letters from sixth-grade students, delivered before my colleagues learned I was retiring. "Dear Seventh Grade Literacy Teacher," they were addressed, and they contained anticipations and hopes for the next year.

The one on top was written by a boy who described himself as "a loud funny kid" whose high hopes at the beginning of each year never quite worked out. In seventh grade he hoped to be "more neater and do all my homework." I let out a sigh, put a rubber band around the letters, and moved them to the counter. Come September, some other teacher at my desk would meet this Huckleberry Finn.

My mind was wandering now, and I felt a bit like one of those kids who came back to visit. Like me now, they would glide around the room touching the lockers, scanning the assignment board. They'd ask whether we still read a book they really liked or did the vocabulary program they hated. It occurred to me that some could remember, could call back, the days before their caterpillar-to-butterfly change.

When Emily, the TV anchor, dropped in and dazzled the kids, she explained that it had taken time for her to make sense of school. But once she discovered her passion for television, she was on fire to learn.

"I knew what I wanted and nothing could get in my way," she said. When she asked if anybody knew what careers they could imagine for themselves, Caleb blurted he was going to be a surgeon so he could make a lot of money. That way, he explained, he could stop working and play video games.

"Why not go straight to designing video games instead?" You could almost see the thought planting itself in his head. "Do what you love," she said.

My mind moved on to another former student, a boy I remembered because of his green bangs. His name was Pablo and in an email he wrote, "You may be surprised that I want to be a teacher." It was his last year in high school and as a senior project, he asked to shadow me for a few weeks in the seventh grade classroom that he said had changed him.

Outside the window of that classroom now, leaves tilted in the late afternoon breeze. I tried to memorize the slanting tree-line. I had gazed into those green depths so many times at the end of a school day, pondering that day's chapter in the lives of the kids, hundreds of them over the years, who had filled these desks.

Slowly I returned to the present and realized the rest of the building was nearly empty. Everyone had gone to the end-of-year party across town. Here I was, surrounded by papers and journals that I couldn't seem to let go of.

Just then there was a knock. A strapping young man was leaning against the door frame, smiling. He had a name tag that I couldn't read from across the room.

"Hi," he said.

He had a goatee and a baseball cap on backwards. He looked nothing like the 13-year-olds I knew so well. But there was something in his smile. Wasn't he the boy with the cowlick who had sat right over there? The one who used to pretend he was reading his book? Like the rest, I knew him so well then. He had to be in college now. How old was he now? Who was he now?

The deep voice spoke again: "Remember me?"

Well, I thought, it's a long story.

# Acknowledgments

Let me start by offering 1,613 thank yous—to my students. Five classes a day with about 25 kids in each for 13 years actually comes to about 1,625. I'm leaving out about a dozen. (You know who you are.) Seriously, my eternal gratitude goes to all the kids who made me part of their story.

Here's to the family that is a school, those folks in the trenches I laughed with and sometimes cried with through the years: fellow teachers, administrators, counselors, colleagues who became friends, too many to name.

The solitary act of writing a book really turns out to be a team project. Two top members of my team—irreplaceable coaches—were my two sisters. My younger sister, Ellen Emerson Yaghjian, was the catalyst from the beginning. Eight years ago, when I talked about attempting a book, she said, "Start now, write things down and send me notes." She kept a file of hundreds of my emails from the classroom, sometimes dashed off just as students were disappearing around the door. She prodded me when I slacked off. Her brainstorming helped lead to a title.

My older sister Laurie Emerson Alexander, an elementary school teacher for decades, was also a special sounding board. She told me stories about kids, gave me advice, guidance, regularly sent research, books and articles that helped me be a better seventh grade teacher.

What you see here is the result of many drafts and many helpful thoughts from readers of the work in progress. First let me mention two Charlies. I was helping organize our 50th high school reunion, which put me in touch with classmates I hadn't seen for a long time. One of them, Charlie Rigano, asked what I'd been up to. When I mentioned this book he offered to be a reader. From there came pages of reactions, memories, and invaluable comments that I incorporated. A second Charlie: Charles Hankey, a friend and neighbor in our community in the Georgia mountains who responded enthusiastically when I mentioned I was writing a book. He asked for a chapter, then the next, and the next. He never asked for a new one without helpfully, thoughtfully commenting on the one he just finished.

An extra special thank you to Margie Wagers. I knew from our years as college roommates she was bright, well-read, astute—and no one gave me better or more useful analysis of my full draft. She made points about phrases she liked or questioned; she led me to go back and fix ambiguities. Her wise insights and frank queries encouraged me and I know made the book better.

Huge thanks to Tom Melham, friend and former National Geographic writer, for an exhaustive, close read with a sharp copy editor's eye.

My gratitude to my pal Leslie Gardner Hankey, Ph.D., for her guidance and bracing enthusiasm over hours and hours, side-by-side, turning manuscript into book.

As time passed, my "team" grew, and I want to thank these individuals for their support (moral, technical and emotional) and valuable and constructive comments: Syd Alexander, Cinda Becker, Stephanie Cooke, Maureen Downey, Bo Emerson, John Emerson, Bella English, Molly Friedrich, Danny Jacobson, Betsy Kiser, Howell Kiser, Mimi Kiser, Kathleen Kryspin, Mary Pigliacelli, Libba Shortridge, Jay Wiggins,

Caroline Alexander Williams, and David Yaghjian.

I've mentioned some family members in the list above. I want to conclude with a few more: First, for raising us in a home that crackled with language and literature and a reverence for words, ideas and curiosity—I must salute my mother, Lucy Kiser Emerson, who could have been the best teacher ever, and my father, William Austin Emerson Jr., in whose footsteps as a journalist and then a teacher I tried to follow. They are the foundation this story is built on.

Thank you to my son Jake for championing me along the way when I was punch-drunk from grading papers into the night and through the weekends, all the while living in the swirl of stories about my hundreds of other "kids." And, years later, for listening to me read my rough drafts with his wife Kelly, both of whom offered perceptive, constructive feedback.

Finally, lucky me, all along I had a professional, live-in editor—my husband, Chris. He knew all the classroom tales through the years and took me seriously when I began to talk about putting them in a book without an outline in mind. He encouraged the initial desire, guided the shape of the project, edited every draft over three years, patiently helped me with pacing ("digress right here"), cutting, adding, proofreading and ultimately helping package the result with a title and cover. A loving thank you to Chris.